MW00848500

BEFORE HASHEM YOU SHALL BE PURIFIED

Rabbi Joseph B. Soloveitchik
on the Days of Awe

Summarized and Annotated by
Arnold Lustiger

Ohr
Publishing

This book was set in 11 pt. Times New Roman by Ohr Publishing, Edison, NJ

First Printing 1998
Second Printing 1999

ISBN 0-9666232-0-7

Contents

v

Prologue

ה' אלוקים דבר מי לא ינבא (עמוס ג:ח)

The Lord God has spoken - who will not prophesy? (Amos 3:8)

The word of Hashem as revealed to the prophet was known as a משא, a "burden." Upon experiencing prophecy, the prophet immediately felt compelled to repeat the message to the people. He found no rest until he fulfilled this task of transmittal, and in this sense the prophecy became a burden that was not lifted until he could share God's word.

In an infinitely more limited sense, we have all shared this sense of burden at one point or another in our lives. Have you ever had the experience of listening to a speaker whose message was so compelling, so sublime, that you felt an urgent need to repeat his remarks to your friends and colleagues?

Whenever one was privileged to hear the Rav זצ"ל at any one of his thousands of public *shiurim* and lectures, this feeling of burden was powerfully evident. After any of his major public presentations, private notes would circulate, to be copied and recopied, ultimately to reach hundreds of people. And although the notes were inevitably but a pale shadow of the majesty of the original lecture, the message still resonated.

There is perhaps some hubris on my part in attempting to summarize the Rav's thoughts on the Days of Awe. In a sense I am like the cantor on the High Holy Days who, in his introductory meditation, suggests that his mission is undertaken even though he is unworthy of the assignment. I was never privileged to be a student of the Rav or to study under any of his students. I therefore have no apparent qualifications to assume this task.

My motivation in writing this summary is solely the sense of burden that compels me to share the thoughts and ideas that so affected me when I heard them. I make this attempt despite the *a priori* realization that, similar to those handwritten notes of the Rav's students of yesteryear, the quality of this presentation does not begin to approach the poetry and drama of the Rav's delivery. Yet, as sterile and dry as these summaries may read compared to the original, I can only pray that the basic rendition still carries something of the essential message that moved me to make this effort.

Acknowledgements

In 1975, I worked as a Materials Engineer at the Frankford Arsenal, a United States government munitions development facility in Philadelphia, where my primary job function was to develop and interpret x-ray diffraction patterns to characterize bazooka shells. It was at that time that *Al HaTeshuvah* was published, and I purchased a copy. So while the x-ray goniometer was generating the texture of slip planes in copper shape charge liners, I was engrossed in this new book.

Al HaTeshuvah left an indelible impression on me. The book combined *peshat* and *derush* infused with a dramatic sweep unlike any work I had ever studied. Every year thereafter, around Rosh Ḥodesh Elul, I would take out my copy of *Al HaTeshuvah*, reread it, and complete it in time for Yom Kippur. Upon finishing the book year after year, I wished to myself that someone would write a sequel.

Years later I moved to Edison, New Jersey and was introduced to Mr. Milton Nordlicht of Queens who maintains a catalog of hundreds of tapes of the Rav's lectures and shiurim. I ordered many of these tapes from him and very quickly became accustomed to having the Rav as a "*ḥavrusah*" during my morning and evening commute.

Among the Nordlicht collection were most of the *teshuvah derashot* of the Rav. As I listened to these tapes, it was evident which of these *derashot* were summarized in *Al HaTeshuvah* and which were not. I took copious notes as I listened to these latter tapes and proceeded to summarize them. Early versions of a few

ix

of these summaries have appeared to members of an Internet mailing list called mail.jewish, moderated by Dr. Avi Feldblum. In addition, a portion of the 1979 *derashah* appeared in the September 1994 issue of *Jewish Action*, published by the Union of Orthodox Jewish Congregations of America.

Upon the appearance of these summaries on the Internet, one of my most frequent e-mail correspondents was Rabbi Shlomo Pick, a rebbe at the Bar-Ilan Kollel and a frequent contributor of articles on the Rav to the Israeli newspaper *Hatzofeh*. I quickly took advantage of his voluminous knowledge to help in identifying uncited references in these and the remaining *derashot*. Rabbi Dov Green of Ḥashmona'im, a very close personal friend as well as a *talmid ḥakham* with great *beki'ut,* provided references to many of these citations as well, and also helped in editing much of the manuscript.

Many others have contributed to this volume. Rabbi Dr. Israel Rivkin provided extensive notes of shiurim and tapes of the Rav. Mr. Robert Kreitman contributed a most interesting insight that I have included as a note in the second chapter. Dr. Chaim Cohen, a linguist at Tel Aviv University, provided the background for an important footnote in the text.

This work would not have been possible without the assistance of my parents ע״מוש, who helped me in translating the more difficult Yiddish words and phrases used by the Rav in these *derashot*. My in-laws ע״מוש have provided the inspiration to embark on this project through their own publishing efforts. Additional thanks go to my brother, Alan Lustiger, for developing three of the fonts that appear in the text.

Dvora Rhein expertly served as overall editor for the manuscript. I wish to acknowledge Mr. Henry Lerner, who selflessly spent many hours reviewing and modifying the manuscript as well. I also thank Rabbi Yaakov Luban of Congregation Ohr Torah and Senior Rabbinic Coordinator at the Orthodox Union for his help and encouragement.

x

Finally, and most importantly, I especially want to express appreciation to my wife for her patience and support as I became increasingly preoccupied with this project. Janice has invested significant time and effort in reviewing each draft and is truly a partner in what has become a labor of love in more than one sense of the term.

Introduction

Between the years 1962 and 1980, Rabbi Joseph B. Soloveitchik *zt"l* ("the Rav") annually delivered a two- to three-hour lecture (*derashah*) in Yiddish between Rosh Hashanah and Yom Kippur on the topic of repentance and the Days of Awe to the Rabbinical Council of America. Most of the *derashot* delivered through 1972 were previously summarized by Rabbi Pinchas Peli in a now classic volume, *Al HaTeshuvah,* which was later translated into English as *On Repentance.* This volume is a summary of the *derashot* that the Rav delivered from 1973 through 1980.

This treatment of these lectures differs from Rabbi Peli's in a number of ways. First, the Rav is mentioned in this work in third person. As a result, all errors in this book should be attributed to me rather than to the Rav. When the Rav is quoted directly, most often in cases of personal reminiscence, his words are indented and set in italics.

Another difference is the use of footnotes and endnotes. Footnotes are used here to document ideas that the Rav himself discussed in the lectures, but were tangential or parenthetical to his main point. Although these ideas were quite compelling in the context of the oral *derashah,* the Rav's essential message might be obscured if they were inserted into the body of the written summaries. Footnotes are also used for citations when the Rav quoted Biblical, Talmudic, or Midrashic sources, whether or not the sources themselves were explicitly mentioned in the lectures. Endnotes are used where specific points in these discourses were reflected in (or, on occasion, contrasted with) other *shiurim* or published works of the Rav, or others' summaries of the Rav's classes and lectures. Endnotes are also used to amplify and/or clarify various points in the *derashot.*

The use of Hebrew characters in the body of each chapter, although not entirely eliminated, is limited in favor of transliteration. Hebrew characters are used in the footnotes and endnotes, as well as in the appendix. In this way the basic message of the Rav could be accessible to an audience that might be unfamiliar with Hebrew or Aramaic, while those who wish to delve deeper into the topics the Rav raised in these discourses can do so through studying the footnotes, endnotes and appendix.

This volume is organized topically rather than chronologically. A footnote at the beginning of each chapter cites the specific year or years of the *teshuvah derashot* upon which the material in that chapter is based. The Table of Contents contains this information for the subheadings in each chapter. Since the topics in each chapter are self-contained, the chapters are not numbered; the reader can feel free to skip chapters to stay current with *inyana deyoma* as the *Yamim Nora'im* progress.

Note that summaries of many of these *derashot* have already appeared in Hebrew dispersed in two books edited by Rabbi Moshe Krona: *Yemei Zikaron* and *Divrei Hashkafah*. Those who compare these summaries with Rabbi Krona's will find that the organization, treatment and detail often vary.

The Jewish community has been anxiously waiting for more of the Rav's Torah to make its way into print. It is my fervent hope that this attempt to present some of the most compelling of the Rav's oral discourses will, to a small extent, meet their expectations. I welcome any comments on this work, and can be reached at: alustig@eclipse.net.

Dr. Arnold Lustiger
Edison, New Jersey
Elul 5758 (August 1998)

Note on the second printing:

This printing includes a new cover design and a few editing changes. In addition, based on numerous requests by readers, we have added an index and list of Biblical, Talmudic and Halakhic citations.

It is with gratitude that I acknowledge the many positive comments received after initial appearance of this book. The need for a second printing is testimony to the enduring interest in the Rav and his thought.

A.L.
Elul 5759 (August 1999)

Thirty years ago, an adolescent having no background in *Gemara* applied for admission to the ninth grade of the Talmudical Yeshiva of Philadelphia. His presence there would be an anomaly since the institution was and remains the most selective of *Yeshivos*. Despite their justified misgivings, the *Roshei Yeshiva* felt that they had no choice but to admit him given the alternative.

Although the student was woefully underprepared, he came under the influence of a Rebbe who displayed a personal warmth that seemed almost otherworldly. Without his inspiration, this boy's Yeshiva experience would have been unimaginably difficult. The concern of this Rebbe for the welfare of his student throughout the student's tenure at the Yeshiva and the years afterward continues to serve as an anchor for his life, even after the Rebbe's untimely passing three years ago.

I am that student. Reb Shimon Sturman זצ"ל was that Rebbe. May his memory strengthen the many hundreds of other students whom he has similarly inspired, and may the knowledge of his continued influence on us comfort his family.

--A. Lustiger

The Message of the Shofar[*]

In his many lectures on *teshuvah*, the Rav often discussed various categories of repentance found in the Gemara and in the Rambam's *Mishneh Torah*, including *teshuvah me'ahavah* (repentance motivated by love) and *teshuvah me'yirah* (repentance motivated by awe);[1] *teshuvah me'ulah* (superior repentance) and *teshuvah she'eino me'ulah* (non-superior repentance).[2] Based on nuances in the wording and the juxtaposition of topics in the Rambam's *Mishneh Torah*, the Rav expanded the Rambam's classifications through the development of categories such as the *teshuvah* of emotion

---

[*] BASED ON THE 1975 *TESHUVAH DERASHAH*

[1] *Yoma* 86b.

[2] Rambam *Hilkhot Teshuvah* 2:1.

versus the *teshuvah* of intellect,[3] and *teshuvah* motivated by conscience versus *teshuvah* motivated by free will.[4]

In his 1975 *teshuvah* lecture, the Rav turned to a somewhat different theme. Instead of introducing new classifications, the Rav defined the various emotional and cognitive stages in the process of *teshuvah*. Each of these stages is reflected as a separate theme defining the respective roles of Rosh Hashanah, the Ten Days of Repentance, and Yom Kippur.

BETWEEN ROSH HASHANAH AND YOM KIPPUR

The Rambam, in *Hilkhot Teshuvah,* utilizes two distinct phrases to refer to the time period spanning Rosh Hashanah and Yom Kippur, commonly known as the Ten Days of Repentance. In the second chapter he writes, "Even though *teshuvah* and supplication are always desirable, in the ten days between Rosh Hashanah and Yom Kippur they are particularly desirable and they are accepted immediately, as it is written: 'Search for the Lord when He can be found...'" (2:6). However, in the very next chapter the Rambam uses a slightly different phrase to describe this time period. The Rambam writes, "Even though the blowing of the shofar on Rosh Hashanah is a decree of the Torah, there is an [additional] inference in it [with the message]: 'Awake sleepers from your sleep and slumberers from your slumber....' Because of this, the entire House of Israel maintains the custom of increasing charity, good deeds, and involvement in mitzvot from Rosh Hashanah until Yom Kippur more than the rest of the year" (3:4).

In delineating a span of time, the words "from" and "until" are not the same as "between" and "and." Biblically,

---

[3] See *On Repentance*, "The Covenant of the Lord."
[4] See *On Repentance*, "The Relationship Between Repentance and Free Choice."

"From...until" generally refers to a geographic or chronological span. For example, in the Biblical passage defining the borders of Israel for the Jewish nation, the Torah states, "Every place that the sole of your foot will walk will be for you, from the desert and Lebanon, from the river Euphrates until the Mediterranean will be your boundaries" (Deuteronomy 11:24). Using "from...until" in this citation, the Torah emphasizes territorial distance. The endpoints serve only as points of reference; in this context "the desert," "Lebanon," "Euphrates," and "Mediterranean" themselves have no individual significance. They are locations meant to delineate a homogeneous distance of space.

In contrast, a phrase incorporating the words "between...and" connotes a different meaning. Examples of two such verses are: "...you shall place it [the *kiyor*] between the Tent of Meeting and the Altar" (Exodus 30:18), and "...he [the angel of God] came between the camp of Egypt and the camp of Israel" (Exodus 14:20). In each of these examples, the emphasis is on the contrast between the boundaries that delineate a location. The endpoints are not mere reference points but actually have significance of their own.

Using these definitions, we can more readily understand the two previously cited *halakhot* of the Rambam.

In the third chapter the Rambam points out that because judgment takes place during the ten days from Rosh Hashanah until Yom Kippur, man finds himself in a position of crisis. He must therefore maximize his performance of mitzvot in order to receive a favorable verdict. The phrase "from...until" suggests that the significance of mitzvah performance is identical during all ten days.

However, in the second chapter, the phrase "between Rosh Hashanah and Yom Kippur" suggests that the nature of "*teshuvah* and supplication" actually differs on Rosh Hashanah, Yom Kippur, and the intervening days. At these specific times of the year, different stages of the *teshuvah* process become operative.

THE DISTANCE BETWEEN GOD AND MAN

The Days of Awe, commencing with Rosh Hashanah, continuing through the Days of Repentance, and culminating on Yom Kippur, is a time period in which we experience a steadily decreasing distance between God and ourselves.

"Your sins have separated between you and your God" (Isaiah 59:2). In the absence of sin, God's presence would be evident in every natural encounter. The whisper of the Master of the Universe would be heard in the bubbling of every crystal spring, His immanence perceived in every sunrise and sunset. Were we not led astray by sin, we would sense God in every breath,[5] in the very rhythm of life. An entire tractate of the Talmud -- the tractate of *Berakhot* -- is dedicated to acknowledging the existence of God in the natural world. A Jew blesses God for providing his mundane needs so as to recognize His presence in everyday life.

The illusion that the world functions autonomously without Divine involvement is a direct result of sin. Correspondingly, the *Shekhinah* or Divine Presence resides in transcendence, removed from creation because of sin. When God is not readily discernible in the world's day-to-day existence, He is known by the Name *E-l* as suggested by the Sabbath tune, "God *(E-l)* is concealed in a hidden abode."[6]

During the course of the year, God in transcendence does not approach us; we must instead seek and find Him. It is through *teshuvah* that man discerns Hashem's presence in the

---

[5] "Every soul (הנשמה) will praise God" (Psalms 150:6): "through every breath (נשימה)" (*Yalkut Shimoni Bereishit*, 20).

[6] R. Avraham Maimon, in the poem recited during *Seudah Shelishit*.

obscuring clouds of the natural world. Despite His great distance from us, we are not free from this imperative: "And from there you will seek Hashem your God, and you will find Him..." (Deuteronomy 4:29). In the *Seliḥot* service we beseech God to "be found as we make our requests," i.e., to make His otherwise obscure presence apparent to us as a result of our supplication.

The paradigmatic figure who found God despite His transcendence is the prophet Ezekiel. Ezekiel's prophetic revelation took place not in the Temple, nor even in the Land of Israel, but rather in a concentration camp in the midst of the bitter Babylonian exile, "among the captives on the River Kevar." Yet, despite the fact that it was a time of acute *hester panim (Deus absconditus)*, "...the heavens opened and [Ezekiel] saw visions of God" (Ezekiel 1:1). When Ezekiel declared: "Blessed is the glory of Hashem from His place" (Ezekiel 3:12), he was referring to the huge distance between God and His people. In contrast, because the prophet Isaiah lived in the Land of Israel during the pre-exilic period, he could speak of God's immanence in this world.[i] Isaiah's declaration, "Holy, Holy, Holy, is the Lord of Hosts, the entire world is filled with His glory" (Isaiah 6:3), was made in close proximity to the spiritual center.[7]

Yet, as Ezekiel demonstrated, God is still accessible despite His distance. The search for the concealed, transcendent God is reflected in the teshuvah obligation which is incumbent upon us throughout the year (Rambam, *Hilkhot Teshuvah* 1:1).

However, as the High Holy Days approach, God's remoteness gradually diminishes. This change in our mutual

---

[7] Ezekiel was figuratively depicted as a villager because of his remoteness from the spiritual center of Jerusalem when God's word was revealed to him. In contrast the prophet Isaiah was described as a city dweller (*Ḥagigah* 13b).

metaphysical-spatial relationship is reflected in the content of our prayers as these days arrive. In the *Shemoneh Esrei* prayer throughout the year, we refer to God as *Ha'E-l HaKadosh* (the Holy God). However, during the Ten Days of Repentance, the phrase *HaMelekh HaKadosh* (the Holy King) is substituted.[8] The appellation *E-l* refers to God in transcendence; God as *E-l* is removed from His creation. In contrast, *Melekh* refers to God Who has a direct relationship to the world, since there is no king without subjects.[9] On Rosh Hashanah, at the time when we first make this change in our reference to Him in prayer, the distance between God and man correspondingly starts to diminish.

THE *TESHUVAH* OF ROSH HASHANAH

According to the Rambam, *teshuvah* has a well-defined and formulated structure. It is a process containing clear strata, involving recognition of sin, remorse, shame, and resolve (Rambam, *Hilkhot Teshuvah* 2:2). There are guideposts in prayer that lead one to engage in this process, as can be found in much of the Yom Kippur liturgy. *Teshuvah* is an all-encompassing activity, engaging man's logic, will, and emotion.

It is therefore surprising to note that there is virtually no reference to sin and forgiveness in the Rosh Hashanah liturgy. There is no recitation of *Seliḥot* (penitential prayer) or *vidui* (confession). Many even have the custom of omitting the first

---

[8] *Berakhot* 12b. The Halakhah considers this change so important, that if one forgets to use the proper phrase, the entire prayer must be repeated (*Oraḥ Ḥayyim* 582:1).

[9] Rabbenu Baḥye, Genesis 39:30. Reflecting this theme, note the phrase in the *Adon Olam* prayer which reads: בעת נעשה בחפצו כל אזי מלך שמו נקרא - "At the time that His Will brought all into being, [only] then was His Name proclaimed as King."

verse of the petitionary prayer *Avinu Malkenu*, "Our Father, Our King, we have sinned before You."

What, then, is the overarching theme of Rosh Hashanah? If *teshuvah* is indeed the theme, how can *teshuvah* take place without explicit reference to sin?

The answer is that on Rosh Hashanah a Jew is involved in a preliminary stage of *teshuvah,* called *hirhur teshuvah* (the "awakening" of *teshuvah*). In contrast to *teshuvah*, the process of *hirhur teshuvah* is amorphous and ill-defined. Yet, despite this lack of definition, *hirhur teshuvah* occupies a special place in Rabbinic thought.

For example, regarding a conditional statement of marriage the Talmud states: "If one says, 'I betroth you on the condition that I am righteous,' even one who is [known to be] absolutely evil is considered betrothed, since perhaps he might be engaged in *hirhur teshuvah* in his heart" (*Kiddushin* 49b). This passage has traditionally posed a difficulty to the Rabbinic commentators. If *teshuvah* is indeed a multistep process, involving sin recognition, remorse, and resolve, how can an individual possibly be considered righteous after only a moment's thought?[ii] Only through *hirhur teshuvah*, which is spontaneous, instinctive, and sudden. In one second, an individual can live the jarring experience of awakening from spiritual somnolence.

A second example of *hirhur teshuvah* is found in the circumstances surrounding the martyrdom of Rabbi Ḥanina Ben Teradion. The Gemara (*Avodah Zarah* 18a) relates that when Rabbi Ḥanina was burned at the stake by the Romans, tufts of wool soaked in water were placed over his heart so as to prolong his agony. The executioner, intensely moved by his suffering, asked of Rabbi Ḥanina whether he could be guaranteed a place in the World to Come were he to remove the tufts of wool and increase the intensity of the fire so as to hasten Rabbi Ḥanina's death. When Rabbi Ḥanina answered affirmatively, the executioner acted accordingly, the latter subsequently hurling himself into the flames as well. At that point a voice from heaven proclaimed that both Rabbi Ḥanina as well as the executioner would enter the World to Come. In response to this Divine verdict, Rabbi Yehudah Hanasi cried, marveling at how some individuals merit the World to Come only after a lifetime of effort, while others acquire such reward after only brief effort.[10]

Why did Rabbi Yehudah Hanasi have such an emotional reaction to the afterlife destiny of the executioner? The answer is that although prior to this incident Rabbi Yehudah Hanasi had understood the redemptive power of *teshuvah*, he had not previously appreciated the redemptive power of *hirhur teshuvah*.

Many mitzvot in the Torah involve an objective act coupled with a subjective component.[iii] The recitation of the *Shema*, for example, involves both the act of recitation as well as the proper intention, namely accepting the yoke of the Kingdom of Heaven. The mitzvah of hearing the shofar on Rosh Hashanah has a similarly dual nature. One is not only obligated to hear the shofar blast, but he must also experience the jarring awakening associated with *hirhur teshuvah*.

Precisely what is involved in the emotional experience of *hirhur teshuvah*? The Rav said that while abstract concepts are often easily described, it is far more difficult to convey such a subjective emotional experience. He therefore felt reluctantly compelled to relate the following personal occurrence as an analogy to clarify this concept:

> *On the seventh day of Pesach, 5727 [1967], I awoke from a fitful sleep. A thunderstorm was raging outside,*

---

[10] The Rav emphasized that the executioner not only earned a share in the World to Come, but achieved the same level as R. Ḥanina in this regard.

and the wind and rain blew angrily through the window of my room. Half awake, I quickly jumped to my feet and closed the window. I then thought to myself that my wife was sleeping downstairs in the sun room next to the parlor, and I remembered that the window was left open there as well. She could catch pneumonia, which in her weakened physical condition would be devastating.[11]

I ran downstairs, rushed into her room, and slammed the window shut. I then turned around to see whether she had awoken from the storm or if she was still sleeping. I found the room empty, the couch where she slept neatly covered.

In reality she had passed away the previous month.

The most tragic and frightening experience was the shock that I encountered in that half second when I turned from the window to find the room empty. I was certain that a few hours earlier I had been speaking with her, and that at about 10 o'clock she had said good night and retired to her room. I could not understand why the room was empty. I thought to myself, "I just spoke with her. I just said good night to her. Where is she?"

Every Jew is obligated to sustain similar emotions on Rosh Hashanah. The required response to the shofar, which the Rambam refers to as awakening from sleep, is the abrupt, tragic realization that the false assumptions upon which we build our lives have come crashing before our eyes. We are jolted with the sudden awareness of the grievous extent to which our actions have alienated us from God. Amidst the panic of this

---

[11] Rebbetzin Tonya Soloveitchik had been suffering from terminal cancer.

experience, we have neither the intellectual nor the emotional fortitude to adequately express remorse, resolve, confession, or even prayer. We find ourselves alone, bereft of our illusions, terrified and paralyzed before God.

In the Book of Judges, the story is told of the decisive military defeat and the humiliating death of the pagan general Sisera at the hand of the Israelites. In a song of praise for this victory, the prophetess Deborah portrayed the mother of Sisera waiting at her window for her son's victorious return from the battle against the Israelites as he had indeed done so many times in the past (Judges 5:28). Yet, although overtly anticipating her son's triumphant return, in a deep recess of her heart Sisera's mother tragically sensed that this time he was in fact never coming home again. *Tosafot* states that we are obligated to hear a total of 100 shofar blasts on Rosh Hashanah, to parallel the 100 cries of Sisera's mother as she waited in vain at that window.[12] Why does the story of a pagan mother awaiting her barbaric son form the halakhic basis for the required number of shofar sounds that are blown on Rosh Hashanah? Because upon hearing the piercing tones of the shofar, we must experience a similar emotion; as we awaken from spiritual complacency, we must witness our own illusions being relentlessly shattered.

This intense experience results in *pahad,* terror. *Pahad* overwhelms and paralyzes the individual, an experience described in the *U'netaneh Tokef* prayer: "And the great shofar will be sounded and a still, thin voice will be heard, and the angels shake, terror and trembling will seize them."

---

[12] תוס׳ ר״ה לג: ד״ה שיעור תרועה

THE PARADOX OF ROSH HASHANAH

The mood of *paḥad* on Rosh Hashanah is reflected in the well known Midrash: "The ministering angels asked before the Holy One Blessed Be He, 'Why doesn't Israel sing *Hallel* before You on Rosh Hashanah and Yom Kippur?' He said to them: 'The King sits on His throne of judgment, with the books of life and the books of death open before Him, and Israel should sing praise?'" (*Rosh Hashanah* 32b). Thus, the Rambam rules that "Hallel is not said on Rosh Hashanah and Yom Kippur because they are days of repentance, fear, and awe; not of extra happiness" (*Hilkhot Hanukah* 3:6). Due to this profound feeling of *paḥad,* the Rav's great-grandfather, Reb Yosef Dov Halevi Soloveitchik, had a custom of fasting on Rosh Hashanah.[iv]

Yet, paradoxically, Rosh Hashanah is also a day of rejoicing. The Rav recounted how his *ḥeder rebbe* would say that there was no greater joy than placing the crown of kingship on Hashem, as it were, a coronation which takes place on Rosh Hashanah. Due to these conflicting themes, Rosh Hashanah is a far more complex holiday than Yom Kippur.[v]

There is an allusion to this emotional conflict in the final verses of the Psalm recited responsively immediately following the *Amidah* of the evening service. King David announces: "Lift up your heads, O gates, and let the everlasting doors be lifted up, and the King of Glory shall come in. Who is this King of Glory? The Lord strong and mighty, the Lord mighty in battle" (Psalms 24:7-8). Initially, God's dominion is foisted upon man against his will. Hashem rules over the earth whether or not we accept Him as our ruler. The doors are passive, yielding to an omnipotent God whose sheer power subjugates all. Such a king is distant from his subjects; the emotion that is appropriate for this sudden encounter with the King's awesome might is dread. The initial shofar blasts heard on Rosh

Hashanah, the *tekiot demeyushav*, reflect this sense of trepidation. There are no introductory verses of prayer or petition between the blessing and the actual blasts; they come upon us suddenly in a charged atmosphere reflecting our state of *paḥad*.

However, in the two concluding verses of the Psalm there is a subtle change in tone: "Lift up your heads, O gates, lift them up, everlasting doors, and the King of Glory shall come in. Who is this King of Glory? The Lord of Hosts, he is the King of Glory..." (Psalms 24:9-10). Here the gates open of their own volition. The everlasting doors are not flung open by Hashem; they are opened by man who welcomes His entry. Hashem rules with man's consent, as reflected in the Biblical verse, "And He was king in Yeshurun when the heads of the people and the tribes of Israel were gathered together" (Deuteronomy 33:5).

Here the second theme of the holiday of Rosh Hashanah is introduced: joy. This emotion, as a theme of Rosh Hashanah, is discussed by the prophet Nehemiah: "Eat the fat and drink the sweet, and send portions unto them for whom nothing is prepared...for this day is holy unto our Lord...for the joy of the Lord is your strength" (Nehemiah 8:10).

Many *Rishonim* would actually recite the passage reserved for the festivals during the *Amidah* of Rosh Hashanah, "And You have given us, Hashem our God, occasions for happiness, holidays and times for rejoicing, this Day of Remembrance...."[13] Indeed, similar to the festivals, the holiday of Rosh Hashanah annuls periods of mourning due to this aspect of happiness.

The second set of shofar blasts, the *tekiot deme'umad* as heard during the *Musaf* prayer, reflect this mood of happiness. The *Shofarot* section joyfully proclaims: "And on your days of rejoicing and festive occasions you will blow trumpets...."

---

[13] רא"ש ר"ה פ'ד:יד

Similarly, *Malkhuyot* affirms that God's rule will willingly be accepted by mankind: "All inhabitants of the earth will know and recognize that to You will every knee bend."

As this transformation takes place, the emotion of *pahad* gives way to a new, more mature emotion: *yir'ah* or awe.[14][vi] The progression from *pahad* to *yir'ah* is implied in our Rosh Hashanah prayers: "And therefore place Your fear *(pahdekha)* on all Your creations...and You will be held in awe *(veyira'ukha)* by all the creatures." The arousal of *pahad* on Rosh Hashanah is not meant to leave the Jew permanently paralyzed. This powerful and ultimately destructive emotion must be transformed into a mobilizing, constructive force during the days leading up to Yom Kippur. *Yir'ah* suggests reverence and loyalty, as exemplified in the Biblical command, "Every man shall revere *(tira'u)* his mother and father" (Leviticus 19:3). The joyful acceptance of God as our King reflects a process of spiritual maturation in the penitent. *Yir'ah* is not based on a visceral fear, but rather reflects a cognitive understanding of God's power. *Yir'ah* in turn prompts introspection *(heshbon hanefesh)* through the remainder of the intervening days culminating with Yom Kippur. The transformation from *pahad* to *yir'ah* facilitates the necessary progression from *hirhur teshuvah* on Rosh Hashanah to *teshuvah* itself during the remaining days of repentance.

---

[14]The Kabbalists refer to the first day of Rosh Hashanah as *dina takifa*, a harsh judgment, while the second day involved *dina rafia*, a lighter judgment, reflecting these two themes of Rosh Hashanah. (*Zohar*, Volume 3, *Parashat Pinhas*, 231b).

NOTES

[i] See the Rav's essay ובקשתם משם, p. 178, where the declarations of Ezekiel and Isaiah are linked:

מסדרי הקדושה הוסיפו שאלה אחת "משרתיו שואלים זה לזה איה מקום כבודו,"
כלומר על אף נוכחותיו של הקב'ה בכל מקום ובכל עת ובכל שעה, הכל שואלים
איפה הוא, כי הלא יושב בסתר הוא עליון.

[ii] See footnote 119 in *Halakhic Man* (p. 159), where the Rav briefly discusses the implications of this ruling in light of a halakhah in *Mishneh Torah*, which suggests that the marriage is *doubtfully* effective.

[iii] The קיום מצוה-מעשה מצוה dichotomy is a theme which appears repeatedly in the Rav's writing and *shiurim*. See, for example, *On Repentance,* "The Power of Confession," where he suggests that *teshuvah* is the קיום מצוה for the objective act of reciting *vidui*. For a more detailed analysis of this dichotomy in relation to קריאת שמע see also, שיעורים לזכר אבא מרי. Some of the philosphical aspects of the concept are discussed in Besdin: *Reflections of the Rav*, "The First Rebellion Against Torah Authority." For more detail on this theme specific to the mitzvah of shofar, see the next chapter.

[iv] The custom to fast on Rosh Hashanah is discussed in *Oraḥ Ḥayyim* 597.

[v] In the *Yarḥei Kallah* presented in the summer of 1972 (summarized in B.D. Schreiber, *Nora'ot Harav*, Volume 1, Chapter 1), the Rav pointed to a *piyyut* to amplify this theme. Rabbi Elazar Hakallir apprehended the conflicting nature of the day through the words of the *piyyut* recited during the *Amidah* repetition of *Shaḥarit*:

נעלה בדין עלות בתרועה, גיא עם דריה לרועעה

בשופר אפתנו ובברך כריעה, במגינת רעים בגנו אתרועעה

He has ascended in judgment to be exalted through the shofar blast, causing the valley [i.e. earth] and its inhabitants to be shattered.

With shofar I will appease Him and with bended knee, through the shield of the beloved [i.e. the Patriarchs] in His garden I will be befriended.

In a jarring juxtaposition, Rabbi Elazar Hakallir weaves the root of the word for shofar blast, *teruah,* to alternately suggest both God's punishment and His befriending of the Jewish people. (Use of the word *teruah* in the context of friendship also appears in Rashi's comment on the phrase ותרועת מלך בו [Numbers 23:21]).

[vi] The opposing concepts of יראה and פחד are described in *The Rav Speaks: Five Addresses by Rabbi Joseph B. Soloveitchik,* pp. 62-64:

> There is a basic difference between fear and awe. The sensation of fear is a neurotic experience. A person suffering fear is sick. Fear creates feelings of helplessness and failure, incompetence and worthlessness. Awe (יראה) is an entirely different sensation.... Obviously the injunction to hold one's parents in awe refers not to fear but to awesome respect. As opposed to fear, the feeling of awe, of awesome respect, is bound up with the feeling of love. Maimonides (*Yesodei HaTorah* 2:1) connects the love of God with the exalted awe that one bears for Him.
>
> The essential result of awesome respect is compliance, since I am proud to have the opportunity to imitate Him whom I respect, to be His messenger and to do His will.

A similar description appears in ובקשתם משם, p. 173.

Man as Both Subject and Object*

The Brisker school of Lithuanian thought is renowned for precise categorization of halakhic constructs. The most familiar of these categorizations is the *Gavra-Ḥeftza* dichotomy: whether a mitzvah is subject- or object-oriented. In his *teshuvah derashah* of 1974, the Rav expanded the scope of such categorization to describe the fundamental principles that underlie the mitzvah of shofar. He then developed the concept even further to promote a view of the metaphysical effect of sin and repentance on man.

* BASED ON THE 1974 *TESHUVAH DERASHAH*

THE MITZVAH OF SHOFAR: OBJECTIVE AND SUBJECTIVE COMPONENTS

As a prologue to every section of the *Mishneh Torah*, the Rambam lists the mitzvot discussed therein. In his prologue to *Hilkhot Shofar*, the Rambam states that there is a requirement "to hear the sound [*kol*] of the shofar on the first of Tishrei," and, in the very first paragraph of the first chapter, he writes that "it is a positive Biblical mitzvah to hear the blast [*teruah*] of the shofar on Rosh Hashanah as the verse states: 'A day of *teruah* shall it be for you.'" Noting two subtle differences in wording between the prologue and the first sentence, the Rav asks: 1) Why does the Rambam use both *kol* and *teruah* to refer to the sound emanating from the shofar? 2) Why does he refer to the day alternately as "the first of Tishrei" and "Rosh Hashanah"?

The answer to both questions lies in understanding the dual aspect of the mitzvah, as outlined by the Rambam: "Even though the blowing of the shofar on Rosh Hashanah is a decree of the Torah, there is an [additional] inference in it [with the message]: 'Awake sleepers from your sleep and slumberers from your slumber and search your deeds, return in repentance and remember your Maker'" (*Hilkhot Teshuvah* 3:4). Not only do these words constitute a moral message, but they bear halakhic implications as well. By introducing the "inference," the Rambam suggests a new understanding of the shofar obligation. While mitzvot such as eating matzah on Pesach do not contain any subjective component and demand no reaction to the significance of the physical act,[i] the Rambam emphasizes here that aside from the auditory experience of hearing the shofar, there is also a *kiyum shebalev* aspect of the mitzvah whose fulfillment requires a subjective emotional response.[ii] In delineating the dual aspect of this mitzvah, the Rambam's words are precise: "Even though the blowing of the shofar is a decree of the Torah...," i.e., even though there is an aspect of the mitzvah that is external and objective, "... there is an inference in it," an inner, emotional fulfillment without which one has not truly addressed the obligation inherent in the mitzvah.

The objective and subjective components of the mitzvah of shofar are indicated by the Biblical phrases *yom teruah* and *zikhron teruah,* respectively. *Yom teruah* refers to the objective component of the mitzvah, and legislates that anyone who hears the necessary shofar blasts fulfills the obligation, even if that person had no intention to fulfill such an obligation. However, the *zikhron teruah* aspect involves a qualitative dimension, a cognitive response. One who has greater understanding of the significance of the shofar blasts and is deeply affected by the majesty and awe engendered by its sound, achieves a greater fulfillment of the mitzvah.[1]

---

[1] At this point, the Rav cited another proof to the objective and subjective components of the mitzvah of shofar. Rava in *Rosh Hashanah* 28a-b states that a *toke'a lashir*, one who blows shofar because he enjoys the sound (as opposed to having in mind fulfillment of the mitzvah) can in fact fulfill his obligation for hearing the shofar in this way. The Gemara states that this is so even despite the requirement for *zikhron teruah*, and that under these conditions the person who is blowing is considered as if he is a *mitasek*, as one who blew a shofar by accident, intending to do something else. The Gemara is difficult to understand, since a true *mitasek* would in fact not fulfill his obligation towards hearing the shofar, as opposed to a *toke'a lashir*. However, in light of the dual nature of the mitzvah these passages can be understood. The difference between a *mitasek* and *toke'a lashir* is only of significance with respect to the objective component of the mitzvah of blowing shofar. Regarding the subjective element of the mitzvah, the person's mind is not concentrating on the meaning of the mitzvah in either case. A *toke'a lashir* is therefore indeed equivalent to a *mitasek* in regard to the subjective component of the *mitzvat shofar*, because the inner fufillment (the *zikhron teruah*) is lacking in both cases.

The differences in wording between the Rambam's introduction and his first paragraph can now be understood. The Rambam, by his use of the phrase "to hear the sound *[kol]* of the shofar on the first of Tishrei" refers only to the aspect of the *mitzvat shofar* dealing with the physical act. Even the day of Rosh Hashanah itself is only sterilely mentioned as a specific day on the calendar to emphasize the mechanical performance underlying the mitzvah. However, when the Rambam states: "It is a positive Biblical mitzvah to hear the blast *[teruah]* of the shofar on Rosh Hashanah as the verse states: 'a day of *teruah* shall it be for you,'" he is alluding to the inner fulfillment. As a result, the Rambam uses the word *teruah* to denote the sound of the shofar, evocative of the trumpet blast which is mandated at a time of communal danger: "And when you go to war in your land against the adversary that oppresses you, then you should blow [a *teruah* blast] with the trumpets" (Numbers 10:9).

The word *teruah* is used when the trumpet is blown in a moment of crisis. Man is conscious of this day not merely as a specific occasion on the calendar when a mechanical act is performed, but as the day of judgment in which man engages in prayer to plead for his life. The Rambam therefore uses the specific name for the holiday which evokes this consciousness: Rosh Hashanah.

One indication that the mitzvah of shofar indeed contains such a subjective component is the close halakhic relationship between blowing the shofar and praying. Although there are two sets of shofar blasts heard on Rosh Hashanah -- the *tekiot demeyushav* (the shofar blasts blown prior to the *Musaf* service) and the *tekiot deme'umad* (those blown during the recitation of *Musaf)* -- Rashi states that the Biblical obligation is not fulfilled until one has heard the latter.[iii]

The integral relationship between prayer and shofar suggests that the highly subjective and emotional prayer

experience *(avodah shebalev[2])* must be paralleled by a similar
sensitivity regarding shofar. Verbally formulated prayer must be
synthesized with a second type of prayer, that which emerges
from the sound of the shofar. As a result, there are a number of
close parallels between the mitzvah of shofar and the mitzvah of
prayer. For example, at the conclusion of the Rosh Hashanah
Shemoneh Esrei, we recite, "For You listen to the sound of the
shofar and are attentive to *teruah*." Our request that Hashem
listen to the shofar blast is worded in language analogous to the
request in the *Seliḥot* penitential: "Listener of prayer, unto You
all flesh comes" (Psalms 65:3). Similarly, the Talmud relates
that, "[the] shofar, since it is made to be a memorial *(zikhron)*,
it is as if it is in the Holy of Holies [of the Temple]" (*Rosh
Hashanah* 26a). King Solomon, in his dedication of the Temple,
identified the direction of prayer as well by way of the Temple
(I Kings 8).

This concept enables new light to be shed on an apparent
conflict between two passages in Tractate *Rosh Hashanah*. In
one mishnah it is ruled that: "All shofar horns are valid [for the
mitzvah] except that of a cow" (*Rosh Hashanah* 26a), while in
another mishnah an apparently different assertion appears:
"Rabbi Yehudah says, 'On Rosh Hashanah a shofar of a ram
must be used.'" (*Rosh Hashanah* 26b). Rabbi Levi explains in
the Gemara that Rabbi Yehudah's statement means that the
shofar should be bent. If virtually all varieties of horns are
valid, how can they be limited by shape?[3] The Rambam, ruling
according to the second opinion, writes: "And the shofar that is

---

[2] *Mekhilta DeRabbi Shimon Bar Yoḥai* 23:25, *Rambam Hilkhot
Tefillah* 1:1.

[3] *Tosafot Rosh Hashanah* 26b: s.v. *shel ya'el pashut* in response to this
apparent conflict, suggests two approaches: 1) the second mishnah is
le'ḥatkhilah while the first is *bedi'eved*, or 2) these two *mishnayot*
constitute a difference of opinion.

blown, whether on Rosh Hashanah or on Jubliee, must be a bent horn of a sheep, and all shofars are invalid except for the horn of a sheep" (*Hilkhot Shofar* 1:1). The Gemara cited above, explaining the requirement for the shofar to be bent, states: "The more a person bends his will, the better," and Rashi elaborates: "His face towards the ground is preferable because of the verse 'and my eyes and heart are there' (I Kings 9:3). Therefore, on Rosh Hashanah when [the shofar] is used for prayer, and to recount the sacrifice of Isaac, it is required to be bent."

The halakhic specification of the shofar's shape suggests that prayer is a critical motif underlying the performance of this mitzvah,[4] reinforcing the integral relationship between prayer and shofar.[iv]

---

[4] However, if a *toke'a lashir* indeed fulfills the objective *yom teruah* component of his shofar obligation, why should this fulfillment not be applied to one who blows a straight shofar? The answer is that if the shofar itself is not an object through which one can fulfill the complete shofar obligation of *zikhron teruah* as well as *yom teruah*, then that shofar cannot allow fulfillment of even the *yom teruah* aspect of the mitzvah. A similar concept applies for the mitzvah of *lulav*: one actually fulfills the mitzvah of *lulav* by simply taking hold of the four species – the shaking sequence (*na'anuim*) normally associated with the mitzvah is not actually required. However, if the *lulav* for some reason is incapable of being shaken, the *lulav* itself is considered deficient and one cannot fulfill the mitzvah through taking such a *lulav*.

THE DUAL NATURE OF PRAYER

The close relationship between prayer and shofar is reflected in how one should approach the act of prayer itself. The *kiyum shebalev* of prayer rests on the absolute dependence of man on the Creator. As such, prayer is not an exclusively Jewish but rather a universal need. Thus, when King Solomon dedicated the first Temple, he specifically included the non-Jew in the prayer community: "And also the non-Jew that will come from a distant land...will come and pray in this house" (I Kings 8:41-42). If a person feels no such dependence on his Creator his very humanity is critically lacking. Prayer is a natural and universal impulse: "As a hart pants for brooks of water, so my soul yearns for you, Lord" (Psalms 42:2).

Prayer is normally associated with speech, the one attribute which differentiates man from other life forms. Via prayer, man represents himself, utilizing the very attribute which attests to his greatness. Man stands before the Creator and engages in conversation in accord with the verse, "A prayer of the afflicted when he faints and pours out his plaint (*siho* - literally 'his conversation') before the Lord" (Psalms 102:1). Man, with his capability of achieving prophecy, engages Hashem in dialogue through verbal prayer.

Yet, not only man engages in prayer. "Hearer of prayer, unto You *all* flesh will come" (Psalms 65:3). All living creatures engage in this activity, instinctively pouring out their needs to God. The mystics consider the chirping of the birds and the cry of the jackal as instinctive sounds uniting them in prayer to their Maker.

When a Jew prays, he must identify himself not only as the very crown of creation who can express himself verbally, but at the same time as a simple life form with mundane but very real physical needs. For the Jew, the wordless cry expresses itself best in the sound of the shofar; hence the halakhic link between shofar and prayer.

In which of these two aspects of prayer must man engage first: well formulated verbal prayer, or instinctive, nonverbal prayer? The Rosh Hashanah service, in which the *Malkhuyot, Zikhronot,* and *Shofarot* sections are recited respectively, each subsequently followed by the shofar blasts, clearly indicates that the verbal precedes the nonverbal.

This sequence reflects a frustration with the inadequacy of verbal prayer. As one example, the Rav said that on Yom Kippur, at the conclusion of the *Ne'ilah* service, he often felt that despite having spent the entire day in prayer, he had not articulated even a tiny fraction of what he wanted to express. This perspective is found within the *Ne'ilah* prayer itself: "The needs of Your nation is great, yet they are lacking in intellect [i.e. the ability to express these needs]."

To illustrate this point, one can imagine that if a father is absent from home for an extended period of time, his son fantasizes that upon his father's return he will relate all of what has transpired in detail during his father's long absence. However, in the excitement and tension of reunion, the son forgets the myriad of detail that he had eagerly anticipated relating; he articulates only disorganized and fragmented ideas.

A Jew has similar feelings at the conclusion of *Ne'ilah,* the final prayer on Yom Kippur: he has spoken, yet said nothing. In order to adequately express his deep longing when words have cruelly failed him, he feels the compulsion to release an instinctive, inarticulate cry. In the seconds before the Holy One Blessed Be He once again retreats into obscuring clouds, man must urgently express what he could not verbalize in an entire day of prayer. He thus sounds the shofar as a response to the ultimate futility of verbal prayer to express his needs.

The constrained nature of prayer in describing man's needs is doubly true when attempting to glorify God. The series of praises which initiate the morning service (*Pesukei Dezimrah*) starts with *Barukh She'amar*, in which we initially express confidence and optimism that our praise and song will be adequate:

> Blessed are You, Hashem, our God, King of the Universe...Who is lauded by the mouth of His people, praised and glorified by the tongue of His devout ones and His servants...We shall exalt You, praise You, Hashem our God, with praises and songs. We shall exalt You, praise You, glorify You, mention Your Name and proclaim Your reign....

However, as the *Pesukei Dezimrah* progress, the more the abject inadequacy of our words to even begin to express God's praise becomes apparent.[v] This theme finds expression in the concluding prayer of *Pesukei Dezimrah*: namely *Yishtabah*. Man understands that despite all the previous praise, he has in a real sense accomplished and said nothing. Hence, as the Kabbalists explain, *Yishtabah* means that God's true praise can only emanate from God Himself: the word *Yishtabah* is a passive verb meaning "may Your Name be praised forever." Its conclusion states, "For You is fitting...song and praise, lauding and hymns...." It would be audacious to suggest that *we* have just engaged in God's praise.[vi] We emphasize that Hashem is "God of Thanksgivings, Master of Wonders, Who chooses musical songs of praise...." He is above the praise of mankind. The only reason we are permitted to even brazenly make the attempt is because God Himself, "chooses musical songs of praise...." In His infinite mercy, God allows us to praise Him despite the feebleness of our attempt.

MAN'S SPLIT PERSONALITY

When discussing the *kiyum shebalev* of shofar, the Rambam lingers on the reproof that is inherent in its sound ("awake sleepers from your slumber").

The communal blowing of the trumpet at a time of collective danger (Numbers 10:9) is executed by the leaders of Israel, who thus reprove, while the masses hear the sound and accept the reprimand. However, when an individual blows the shofar on Rosh Hashanah on his own behalf in order to fulfill the mitzvah, to whom is the message of the shofar directed? In other words, who is the "reprover" and who is the "reproven"?

The answer can be inferred from a passage in Tractate *Rosh Hashanah*:

> The Rabbis stated: "The following are obligated in the blowing of the shofar: priests, Levites, and Israelites, strangers, freed slaves, hermaphrodites, those castrated and half-slaves. One who is half-slave cannot blow on behalf of those of his own kind or those not of his kind." Rav Huna states that for himself he can blow. Rav Naḥman responded to Rav Huna: "What is the difference between blowing for himself and blowing for others? Just as the part of himself that is a slave cannot allow others to fulfill their obligation [when the half-slave blows the shofar on another's behalf], similarly the part of himself that is a slave cannot allow the free half of himself to fulfill his obligation." Rav Naḥman [therefore] said that he cannot blow even for himself (*Rosh Hashanah* 29a).

One who is not obligated to execute a mitzvah himself cannot be the cause of fulfillment for another who is obligated. A slave therefore cannot blow shofar on behalf of a free man because the slave is exempt from the mitzvah. Similarly, a half-slave cannot blow shofar on behalf of a free man; because the part of him that is a slave cannot blow on behalf of someone who is free. Furthermore, a half-slave cannot blow shofar on behalf of another half-slave, because the part of him that is a slave cannot blow on behalf of the part of another that is free. Rabbi Naḥman goes even further to state that the half-slave cannot even blow shofar on his own behalf, since the act of blowing is partially being accomplished by the part of the individual that is a slave, i.e. a part of him that is unable to exempt his own free part.

Rabbi Naḥman's opinion would seem to fly in the face of common sense. For example, what does a half-slave do when it comes to other mitzvot that only free men are obligated to perform? Prayer, *tzitzit*, *tefillin* or *lulav*, are all mitzvot that the half-slave is required to perform, ignoring the half that is not obligated! Why, then, should shofar be different from these other mitzvot?

The answer is that the actual mitzvah of shofar is not in the blowing but in the hearing. The blessing recited before the first shofar blasts states: "...Who has sanctified us with His mitzvot and commanded us to *hear* the sound of the shofar." He who blows the shofar creates a sound in which others, as well as himself, can fulfill the mitzvah. Inherent in the mitzvah of shofar is the participation of two types of individuals: a *toke'a* (blower) and a *shome'a* (listener). For the other mitzvot enumerated, such as donning *tallit* and *tefillin*, there is no demonstrative aspect at all. One fulfills the obligation through the act of the mitzvah itself.

In light of this halakhic construct, we can now offer an approach to who provides the reproof and who is the reproven. It would appear that the mitzvah of shofar conceptually splits the person who blows it into both a *toke'a* and *shome'a*, an active and passive participant. When an individual is both a *toke'a* and *shome'a*, the individual is speaking to himself. The mitzvah of shofar thus expresses itself as a dialogue between two personalities within. As one talks, the other listens.

In a strict sense, however, it is incorrect to state that the mitzvah of shofar itself splits a personality in this way. Mitzvot in fact do just the opposite by uniting the whole personality. Fulfillment of Torah unites a split, scattered personality into a coherent whole. The *Shemoneh Esrei* prayer which includes the hope of "gathering the dispersed of Israel" addresses an imperative on an individual as well as a communal level.[vii]

Instead, the bifurcation of personality occurs not through mitzvot, but rather through sin. Sin splits the personality into *tamei* (impure) and *tahor* (pure) components. Judaism desires the unity of the individual, in keeping with the imperative to maintain the image of God. *Imitatio Dei* is the foundation of human existence. Since Hashem is One, our own goal must be to emulate this attribute as closely as possible. The Torah never accepted the dictum that the body is intrinsically impure: on the contrary, man must strive towards sanctification of the body. Judaism desires that man be internally consistent, without conflict or contradictions.

In a sense, we are fortunate that sin performs this function of splitting the human personality, for otherwise, the entire personality would become enveloped in impurity. If the whole personality would be corrupt, it would be impossible to engage in *teshuvah*. Repentance cannot be *creatio ex nihilo:* it can be mobilized only from an initially uncorrupted core. Even in the most egregious of transgressors, something pure remains. Judaism does not believe in the modern theory that there are irredeemable criminals doomed to spend their lives in sin. Even Jeroboam, the greatest sinner of all, as well as Elisha ben Abuya, were told *ḥazor bakh* -- return (Sanhedrin 102a). A fundamentally impure personality cannot effect such a return. The split in personality is what makes *teshuvah* possible.[5]

---

[5] The equation between sin and separation is a theme in Kabbalah as well. Sin results in the separation of the attribute of *malkhut* from

The shofar therefore addresses itself to the split personality of the sinner. The pure part of this personality provides reproof, while the impure part listens. In effect, the shofar tells the person that the sinner can only speak in the name of a portion of the personality, not the whole person.

The message of the shofar, that the impure side of the personality does not represent the entire individual, is part of what the Rambam calls the "story of the exodus from sin." In one of his recorded letters, the Rambam draws an analogy between *teshuvah*, the exodus from sin, and the exodus from Egypt. In this conception, the person is a slave to the sinful aspect of his personality, while *teshuvah* is the redemption. Just as on Pesach we must engage in telling the story of the exodus from Egypt, on Rosh Hashanah we must also engage in telling the story of the exodus from sin. The medium through which this story is told is the shofar. The message to the sinner is that there is an inner, pure part to his personality which is "in exile," and that the sinner is acting as a false witness if he represents himself as the entire individual.

THE VARIOUS ROLES OF MAN

Man as Subject - *Nosei*

The concept of man as both *toke'a* and *shome'a* regarding the mitzvah of shofar can be generalized and is applicable to many things. In everyday language, we often refer to people or items as subjects or as objects. For example, if one writes a letter, the writer is the subject. He is engaged in a creative activity, while the letter is a passive object, the item being acted

---

yesod: between the Divinity manifest in nature and the Divine spark revealed to people through the soul (*Zohar*, Volume 3, *Pinḥas* 131b).[xi]

upon. This simple concept is applicable to virtually anything in the world.

The categories of subject and object are used extensively as well in the world of Halakhah. As only one of many examples, the difference between making a vow *(neder)* and swearing *(shevuah)* rests on this dichotomy. *Shevuah* involves what is known as an *issur gavra*, a prohibition which is dependent on the subject. One can swear not to sit in a sukkah, for example, the emphasis being on the individual to whom the prohibition is directed ("*I* swear not to sit in that sukkah"). *Neder,* on the other hand, is a formulation which rests on the object being prohibited, an *issur ḥeftza* ("That sukkah is prohibited to me").

On a metaphysical level, one can conceptualize Hashem as a *nosei* -- a subject in the most absolute sense. His omnipotence is expressed in a number of ways: the creator of worlds, the *Ein Sof.* Hashem continually renews His creation *(meḥadesh betuvo bekhol yom tamid ma'aseh bereshit)* such that our very world depends on His constant involvement as Creator.

Man, created in His image, crowned with honor, was given the imperative to walk in His ways -- *vehalakhta bidrakhav.*[6] Explaining this imperative, the Rambam (in the introduction to *Hilkhot De'ot)* uses the expression *lehidamot lo* -- to imitate Him. The Rav says that imitation of Hashem is not limited to performing acts of compassion *(Masekhet Smakhot Evel Rabati* 6:1), but extends to imitation of the essential attribute of becoming a *nosei.* In keeping with this imperative, man must therefore strive to become subject and not object *(nisa)*, one who influences one's surroundings *(mashpia)* rather than one who is influenced *(mushpa)*, one who creates and is not

---

[6] This thought is also expressed in Rashi's interpretation of the phrase *zeh E-li ve'anvehu* (Exodus 15:3). The word *ve'anvehu* is a contraction of the words *ani vehu*: "I and He" -- *mah hu af ani (Rashi Shabbat* 133b s.v. *hevei domeh lo).*

created, one who acts and is not acted upon, one who controls his environment rather than being controlled by it.

A person as subject is blessed with free will. This gift was not given to inanimate objects because their essential nature is that they are passive. Free will allows man to fulfill his role as a subject.

In light of this distinction, we can define sin in these simple terms. Sin occurs when man becomes an object, when he changes from *gavra* to *heftza*, when he is transformed from a creator to a victim.

The simplest verbs which denote the dichotomy between a subject and an object are those of ascent and descent, respectively. Ascent involves an act of overcoming the force of gravity, while descent involves succumbing to this force. Gravity is a force that is not characteristic of personality, it is characteristic of objects, things. If a person loses his dynamic, subjective existence and cannot counteract various forces which tend to pull him downward, he is acting as a simple object.

Not coincidentally, ascent and descent are Biblical metaphors for mitzvah and sin, respectively. When Israel sinned during the Golden Calf incident, Hashem's instructions were for Moses to descend Mount Sinai, while upon his reacceptance of the Tablets, the command was for Moses to ascend. The breaking of the Tablets as an expression of Israel's sin reflects the metaphor of descent, commemorated on the 17th day of Tammuz when Moses was commanded, "Go descend" (Exodus 32:7). In contrast, the reestablishment of the Tablets commemorated on Yom Kippur, involving an act of self-creation as Moses himself hewed the tablets (Exodus 34:1), reflects the metaphor of ascent ("Ascend Mount Sinai in the morning" [Exodus 34:2]). Ascent is also closely associated with Jerusalem and the Temple: "You shall arise and ascend to the place which the Lord your God has chosen" (Deuteronomy 17:8).

In the Yom Kippur Temple service (the *Avodah*), the object most closely identified with sin is the *sa'ir hamishtalei'aḥ*, the scapegoat. The mishnah in *Yoma* describes the ultimate fate of the scapegoat in the ritual: "It went backward, and it rolled and descended until it was halfway down the mountain, where it became dismembered into many parts" (*Yoma* 67a).

Can there be a more accurate description of what sin itself does to a person? Even before his total descent he is broken apart, an abject victim of gravity.

Sin transforms a person into someone who is acted upon or influenced. In response to the very first sin, when Hashem confronted Adam after eating from the tree of knowledge, Adam's response was, "The woman who You gave to be with me, she gave it to me..." (Genesis 3:12). When Hashem confronted Eve in turn, the response was similar, "The snake tricked me and I ate" (Genesis 3:13). Both emphasized their helplessness in overcoming an external influence that "forced" their fall. Suddenly, man as the crown of creation, sent forth to conquer the earth ("fill the earth and conquer it" [Genesis 1:28]) succumbed to the very environment he was created to control.

Regarding sin, an analogy is made to sleep. Sleep is an absolute passive state, in which man is pure object. The insistent demand of the shofar, according to the Rambam, is the imperative to awaken oneself. When he is awake, man can protect himself and control his environment, but he is powerless when sleeping.

A Biblical account making the equation of sin with sleep is found in the incident of Samson and Delilah. Samson had a unique personality, fundamentally different from the other national leaders, or judges, of his time. All the other judges: Deborah, Barak, Gideon, Jephthah, were great leaders of people. They led armies to war and were fine strategists. They could be categorized as leaders or commanders. However, only

Samson was called *gibor*, mighty. He acted against his enemies as a solitary figure; he needed no one to abet him in his battles.

The account in the Book of Judges emphasizes the terror that Samson struck in the hearts of the Philistines. Physical strength alone is inadequate to explain this reaction on the part of his enemies. One individual, no matter how strong, could never defeat thousands of people on the basis of physical might alone. The power of Samson over his enemies emanated from a deeper, psychological source. His unique abilities stemmed from a dynamic, spiritual personality, a personality which paralyzed others in confrontation. His enemies did not understand the power that he held over them, and they asked Delilah to ascertain the secret.

Yet, when Samson fell asleep on the lap of Delilah, he was suddenly transformed -- he lost his role as subject and became object. The stunning tragedy of this transformation was Samson's total lack of awareness that this change had even taken place. After his fateful sleep, he awoke and said: "'I will go out as usual,' but he did not know that God was removed from him" (Judges 16:20).

The lack of awareness that one has lost his dynamic personality is the ultimate tragedy of all sinners.[7] Sometimes Delilah is a vulgar type of beauty, sometimes she is a community, sometimes a political system, or the search for hedoné. Every

---

[7] The Rav took the story of Samson's unawareness of his loss of strength as an analogy to the State of Israel's reaction during the Yom Kippur War of 1973. In the initial days of the war, hubris resulted in the belief that the war would be won in a few short days, similar to the Six-Day War of 1967. Only after the war became extended and the news of battlefield losses mounted was there even an awareness of vulnerability. The Rav stated that the "Delilah" in the case of the State of Israel was widespread belief in the Land of Israel without the God of Israel.

generation has its own temptation which reduces individuals to the level of object.

What, therefore, is *teshuvah* in contrast to sin? Ascent versus descent. Through sin one is an object, while *teshuvah* allows one to again become a subject. Through sin man is acted upon, while through *teshuvah* man can act once again. Through sin he is a thing, while through *teshuvah* he becomes a person. Through sin gravity overwhelms, while through *teshuvah* gravity is overcome. When Israel sinned, gravity overcame Moses, who could not support the first set of Tablets. When Israel then returned in *teshuvah*, gravity was overcome and the second Tablets were indeed held high.[viii]

The shofar must serve as the alarm which warns man that because of sin he is pulled ever downward, staring into an abyss. He must heed the cry of the shofar and engage in *teshuvah* in order to regain his dynamic personality.

Man as Object - *Nisa*

Although Hashem as Creator is absolute *nosei*, there are occasions, paradoxically, when God acts as one who can be influenced, as *nisa*. This attribute is specifically evident when we refer to Hashem as One who listens to prayer.

Hashem as both *nosei* and *nisa* is indicated by the proximity of two verses in the psalm comprising most of the *Ashrei* prayer. "Your kingdom is a kingdom that spans all eternities, and Your reign is in every generation" (Psalms 145:13). Hashem's Will leads the entire cosmos. Nothing takes place on earth without His dictate. Through His Will He controls events millions of light years away. Yet, at the same time, "He does the will of those who fear Him, and He will hear their cry and save them" (Psalms 145:19). His Will envelops infinity, yet when it comes to those who follow Him, he "steps aside," as it were, and becomes the *nisa*. Every Jew can pray, can open his heart

from the depths of his being, can make requests of Hashem,
which He can then choose to fulfill. In this way, insignificant
man influences the Omnipotent.

Before man does *teshuvah*, Hashem is distant from him.
During the Ten Days of Repentance, Hashem brings man close
to Him. As such, the one who does *teshuvah* becomes the *nosei*
and Hashem, as it were, becomes the *nisa*. "He does the will of
those who fear Him."

The very concept of prayer is a mystery to the Rabbis. How
is it possible that lowly man can influence the Master of the
Universe through prayer? Yet prayer is the most powerful
weapon in the hands of man, because through prayer, man as
nosei can influence Hashem as *nisa*.

On Rosh Hashanah, Hashem moves from the throne of justice to the throne of mercy. This movement takes place because
man influences while Hashem becomes influenced. This
mysterious notion is the enigmatic result of prayer.

The Rav recounted how, as a child, his teacher in *heder*
would refer to the first night of Rosh Hashanah as "coronation
night," the time at which we crown Hashem as we proclaim our
acceptance of the yoke of heaven. The Rav remembers asking
his teacher why, if Hashem is truly King of the world, does He
need man to place the crown on His head?

The Rav did not understand exactly what the teacher answered at the time, but he did remember him quoting a phrase
from the Song of Songs (7:6): "The king is held captive in the
tresses [of His beloved]."

In the physical universe, Hashem is the *nosei*, but in His relationship with Jewish destiny, Hashem wants the Jew to play
the active role. Regarding Jewish history, Hashem is passive,
nisa, "held captive" as it were.

In light of this concept, the Rav homiletically reinterpreted the
phrase from the Shaḥarit service, *HaMelekh hayoshev al kisei ram
venisa*. This phrase is generally translated: "O King, Who sits upon

a high (*ram*) and lofty (*nisa*) throne." In his homiletical interpretation, the Rav translates it as, "O King, Who sits upon a throne, is *ram venisa*." *Ram* refers to Hashem's absolute control of the cosmos, while *nisa* refers to Hashem's relationship to Jewish destiny as He listens to our entreaties.[ix]

In response to the imperative of *vehalakhta bidrakhav*, we must also assume this dual role. Not only must we play the part of *nosei*, but of *nisa* as well. At specific times, man must be a *mashpia*, at other times a *mushpa*. The shofar, as explained earlier, symbolizes this dual role, as the person blowing the shofar is at the same time a *toke'a* and a *shome'a*.

The very creation of man suggests his dual role. "And the Lord created the man in His own image, in the image of the Lord He created him, male and female he created them" (Genesis 1:27). What is the meaning of the juxtaposition between the image of God and the creation of man as two sexes? The answer is that male and female in this context are to be taken not in a physiological but rather in a spiritual/metaphysical sense. The male aspect refers to man with the dynamic, active personality of a *nosei*, while the female aspect refers to man with the passive personality of a *nisa*.[x] The possession of both qualities, in turn, reflects the image of God Who is *ram venisa*.

As far as man is concerned, the means to achieve the attribute of *ram* is clear. It is imperative to be physically and spiritually powerful -- to be like Samson-- but to wake up at the sound of the shofar before Delilah wakes us....

But in what way does Hashem want man to be a *nisa*? First, through subjugating himself to the Higher Will.

The paradigm of man as both *nosei* and *nisa* was Abraham. On the one hand, he was perhaps the best *nosei* in Jewish history. As a young child, he alone uncovered the secret of the unity of Hashem. The Rambam emphasizes that no one taught him (*Hilkhot Avodah Zarah* 1:3). In addition to his spiritual strength, his physical prowess was demonstrated in his battle with the four kings (Genesis 14).

Yet, upon Hashem's command, this same person took his son to be sacrificed. He did not question the glaring contradiction between God's command and His previous commitment to make Abraham's children into a great nation. By performing the *Akedah,* Abraham was acting against everything he believed. Yet, he bent his own will to Hashem's, thus acting as a *nisa.* During the *Akedah* incident, Abraham told his servants, "I and the lad will go until there and bow..." (Genesis 22:5). The act of bowing symbolizes total subordination to Hashem.[8]

Besides subordination, another manifestation of man as *nisa* is the attribute of sensitivity. When a potential convert approached Hillel and asked him to summarize the entire Torah on one foot, he replied, "What is hateful to you, do not do to your friend" (*Shabbat* 31a).

Insensitivity and cruelty are diametrically opposed to Judaism. A Jew must be merciful and charitable; to see someone else in pain should be unbearable. When Eliezer searched for a wife for Isaac, his criterion was kindness (Rashi on Genesis 24:14, s.v. *attah hohakhta*). Rebecca's response suggested that she had the requisite quality of sensitivity, even towards Eliezer's animals. Only one who displayed these qualities could be a proper wife for Isaac.

A complement to sensitivity is the yearning for holiness. As a small illustration, the Rav used the following anecdote from his past:

---

[8] The Rav stated that the widespread support of the State of Israel by the general Jewish community is a manifestation of man's attribute of *nisa.* Their ongoing support of Israel, a small country whose continued existence defies all odds, is an irrational act that flies in the face of their own natural pragmatism.

Not far from where our family lived there was a Modzitzer shtiebel where I would occasionally go for shalosh seudos. *The ḥasidim would be singing* Bnei Heikhala, Hashem Ro'i Lo Eḥsor, *again* Bnei Heikhala, *again* Hashem Ro'i. *It occurred to me that they weren't singing because they wanted to sing, they were singing because they did not want to allow Shabbos to leave....*

I remember an encounter in this shtiebel *as a small child. One of the men who had been singing most enthusiastically, wearing a* kapota *consisting of more holes than material, approached me and asked if I recognized him. I told him that I did not, and he introduced himself as Yankel the Porter. Now during the week I knew Yankel the Porter as someone very ordinary wearing shabby clothes walking around with a rope. I could not imagine that this individual of such regal bearing could be the same person. Yet on Shabbos he wore a* kapota *and* shtreimel. *That is because his soul wasn't Yankel the Porter, but Yankel the Prince.*

Well after nightfall I naively asked him, "When do we daven Ma'ariv?*" He replied: "Do you miss weekdays that much [that you cannot wait to daven* Ma'ariv*]?"*

The mitzvah of extending Shabbat into the weekday reflects the yearning of the Jew for holiness.

There is a mishnah that amplifies this theme. The mishnah lists a number of individuals who do not merit a share in the World to Come, including Bilam, Do'eg, Aḥitophel, and Geḥazi (*Sanhedrin* 10:2). The evil nature of the first three is well known: Bilam threatened to destroy the nascent Jewish nation even before reaching their soil. Do'eg slaughtered an entire community of priests at Saul's behest. Ahitophel plotted against the kingdom of David through his alliance with Avshalom.

The inclusion of Gehazi in this list seems somewhat out of place. The sin of Gehazi, the servant of the prophet Elisha, was that he coveted a gift that was offered to Elisha but refused by his master. What was the severity of this sin such that he deserved to be listed among this immensely wicked company?

Gehazi's sin lay in the fact that although he served the prophet for so long and was in the very presence of holiness, his fundamental personality remained unaffected. His insensitivity to the personification of sanctity in the person of Elisha, a sanctity to which he had such close proximity and access, placed him on the same level as much more evil people who did not have the benefit of such association. The lack of Elisha's positive influence on his servant stands in stark contrast to Elisha's own metamorphosis as protege to the prophet Elijah, as well as to Joshua's relationship with Moses.

In the *Malkhuyot* portion of the *Amidah* recited on Rosh Hashanah, we ask God to establish His Kingdom on earth, "[so] all children of the flesh (*b'nei basar*) will call upon Your Name, to turn all the wicked of the earth (*rish'ei aretz*) towards You." *B'nei basar*, referring to those who cannot resist sin, will shed the destructive *nisa* aspect of their personalities as they no longer succumb to temptation. The *rish'ei aretz*, evildoers who actively rebel against God, will abandon their insubordinate *nosei* attitude as they subjugate themselves to their Maker. Thus, an important theme of *Malkhuyot* is that we must strive to become *nos'im* in areas that we previously were *nisa'im*, and vice versa.

NOTES

[i] It should be mentioned, however, that the Rav indicated in a number of public lectures that the eating of matzah at the Seder is, in fact, one aspect of the fulfillment of the mitzvah of סיפור יציאת מצרים. The Rav used this idea to explain Rabban Gamliel's statement in the Haggadah.

[ii] As an example of another application of this concept see *On Repentance*, "The Power of Confession," where the Rav discusses the mitzvah of prayer in the context of *kiyum shebalev*.

[iii] The Rav is referring here to Leviticus 23:24, where the term *zikhron teruah* is used. According to Rashi, the term refers to the recitation of the verses of *Zikhronot* and *Shofarot* in *Musaf*. This interpretation suggests that the shofar-blowing (*teruah*) and the recitation of these verses must be closely associated in order for one to fulfill the mitzvah of shofar.

[iv] In the 1970 Yarḥei Kallah, the Rav noted that according to the Yerushalmi, the blessing for shofar is לשמוע בקול שופר: to listen into the sound of the shofar (i.e. so as to prompt the necessary emotional response).

[v] In a lecture presented in Boston on April 18, 1970, the Rav cited *Nishmat*, the penultimate prayer of *Pesukei Dezimrah*, as explicitly expressing this idea:

> ...were our mouth filled with song as the sea with water and our tongue ringing with praise as the roaring waves, were our lips full of adoration as the wide expanse of heaven, and our eyes sparkling like the sun or the moon, were our hands spread out in prayer as the eagles of the sky, and our feet as swift as the deer--we still would be unable to thank You and bless Your Name, Lord our God and God

of our fathers, for even one of the thousand thousands of thousands and myriad myriads of favors that You performed for our ancestors and for us.

Why, then, do we even attempt to praise God? Because, in a sense we cannot help ourselves. As *Nishmat* continues:

> Therefore the limbs which You gave us, the spirit and soul which You breathed into our nostrils, and the tongue which You put in our mouth shall all thank, bless, glorify, extol, revere, hallow, and do homage to Your Name, our King.

[vi] This thought is likewise expressed by Rashi in the *Az Yashir* passage (Exodus 15:11) on the phrase *nora tehillot*, which he translates as "too awesome for praise." In Rashi's words, "People are afraid to tell Your praises lest they be too few, as it is written, 'to You, silence is praise' (Psalms 65:2).

[vii] In a lecture to the Rabbinical Council of America in the mid-1950's, the Rav explained that the Biblical phrase: "אם יהיה נדחך בקצה השמים משם יקבצך... " (דברים ל:ד) is written in the singular because the verse refers to individual rather than communal redemption.

[viii] Although in most midrashic accounts Moses threw the Tablets down in response to Israel's sin, in the account of the *Yalkut Shimoni* (*Ki Tisa* 393) Moses actually dropped the Tablets because they became too heavy for him to bear. According to the Rav, Moses' sudden inability to carry the Tablets reflects Israel's own fall towards sin in the sense of חפצא. In contrast, the second time that Moses climbed Mount Sinai, he was able to ascend the mountain while carrying this new set of Tablets, reflecting Israel's *teshuvah* and their resultant rise as גברא (1964 Yahrtzeit *Shiur*). For a summary of this lecture, see ימי זכרון, chapter on שליחות, pp. 9-28.

This passage in the *Yalkut Shimoni* is also discussed in the Rav's 1979 *teshuvah derashah* in a different context (see the chapter on "The Avodah and the Conclusion of Yom Kippur").

[ix] Although this interpretation is clearly homiletic, it is striking to note that the Rav's interpretation of *nisa* in describing God as One who accepts supplication is quite consistent within the context of those prayers in which the phrase *ram venisa* appears. For example, in the אַרֶשֶׁת שְׂפָתֵינוּ prayer recited immediately after each set of shofar blasts in the *Musaf* of Rosh Hashanah we recite:

אֲרֶשֶׁת שְׂפָתֵינוּ יֶעֱרַב לְפָנֶיךָ קֵל <u>רָם וְנִשָּׂא</u>, מֵבִין וּמַאֲזִין מַבִּיט וּמַקְשִׁיב לְקוֹל תְּקִיעָתֵינוּ וְקַבֵּל בְּרַחֲמִים וּבְרָצוֹן סֵדֶר [מַלְכוּיוֹתֵינוּ/זִכְרוֹנוֹתֵינוּ/שׁוֹפְרוֹתֵינוּ]

May the utterance of our lips be pleasant before You, O God Who is *ram venisa*, Who discerns and gives ear, looks closely and hearkens, to the sound of our shofar blasts, and may You accept with mercy and favor the order of our [*Malkhuyot/ Zikhronot/ Shofarot*] verses.

We ask God, using the appellation *Ram Venisa*, to listen to our prayer. Another example appears in the *Seliḥot* passage מַכְנִיסֵי רַחֲמִים where we exhort the angels:

הִשְׁתַּדְּלוּ וְהַרְבּוּ תְחִנָּה וּבַקָּשָׁה לִפְנֵי מֶלֶךְ קֵל <u>רָם וְנִשָּׂא</u> --

"maximize our supplication and request before the King Who is Lord *Ram Venisa*."

[x] See יְמֵי זִכָּרוֹן, chapter on הַבְּרָכוֹת בַּיַהֲדוּת, pp. 32-37, where the Rav discusses this metaphysical distinction between man and woman in more detail.

[xi] A brief introduction to the Kabbalistic concept of the ten Divine attributes or emanations (the *sefirot*) and how man negatively affects them through sin, appears in Adin Steinsaltz, *The Thirteen Petalled Rose*, (Basic Books, 1980) 35-47.

The *Selihot* Service[*]

THE CONCEPT OF *SELIHOT*

Judaism has always thought of man antithetically, based on two mutually exclusive principles. One concept is that man is an important, powerful, and exalted being, capable of reaching dizzying intellectual and spiritual heights. Man embodies a Divine element that allows him proximity to his Creator. On the other hand, Judaism also perceives man as a worthless, lowly being. Not only is he weak and helpless, but he is capable of becoming morally corrupt, cruel and beastly, defiling both himself and the world. Reflecting this dual perception of man, *Hazal* said: If man is meritorious, he is told, "You have preceded the angels,"

---

[*] BASED ON A 1968 *SHIUR* IN BOSTON AND THE 1978 *TESHUVAH DERASHAH*

and if not, he is told, "a mosquito has preceded you" (*Bereishit Rabbah* 8:1).

The *Amidah* (or *Shemoneh Esrei)* prayer is a reflection of the affirmation of man, based on the awareness of man as a great being. In *Shemoneh Esrei* man approaches God, pleads with Him and engages Him in dialogue. Although we find in *Tanakh* that praying was usually practiced while the worshiper was kneeling or in a position of full prostration, it is interesting to note that when *Ḥazal* introduced prayer they insisted on the opposite posture. To prostrate oneself in *Shemoneh Esrei* would invalidate the prayer; *Shemoneh Esrei* requires standing straight, upright. *Ḥazal* similarly required that one be dressed in his best clothes for prayer. *Ḥazal* interpreted prayer as if it were an audience between the King and some very prominent individual. When praying, man confronts God directly and addresses himself directly to Him, in accordance with the prayer that is said at the concluding *Ne'ilah* prayer on Yom Kippur: "You have separated man from the beginning to stand before You." God has singled out man and has given him the license to approach Him. There is familiarity and intimacy in our approach to God.

On the other hand, there is a different set of prayers that is based on the opposite assumption, the nihility of man. The prayers of *Seliḥot* are predicated on man's worthlessness and weakness, his loneliness and helplessness, of his base nature that allows him to become corrupt and defiled. The *piyyutim* of *Seliḥot* are infused with this one idea: how can lowly man possibly approach God; how can man address himself to Him? In spite of all his progressive ideas, all his technological discoveries, man is defiled, corrupt, ignorant, a prisoner of nature.

The greatness of man is the lodestar of prayer the whole year, while the weakness and helplessness of man is the guiding motif of *Seliḥot*.

Although the Rosh Hashanah and Yom Kippur prayers contain a mixture of these motifs,[i] one of the most explicit expressions of the negative view of man appears in the *U'netaneh Tokef* prayer: "[Man] is likened to a broken shard, a fading flower, a passing shade, a dissipating cloud, a blowing wind, flying dust, and a fleeting dream."

This emphasis, based on the nihility of man, is inevitably associated with the nighttime: man at night is not as proud, not as vain, not as sure of himself as in the daytime. For example, "She weeps bitterly in the night..." (Lamentations 1:2), or, "Arise, cry out at night, at the beginning of the watches" (Lamentations 2:19).

When one is in distress, the experience of sorrow is keener and more painful at night. In contrast, during the daytime one is involved with the creative and positive aspects of man. As a result, the *Rishonim* stipulated that *Seliḥot* should be recited only at night[1] and completed at night, or continued until daybreak ("at the beginning of the watches"), in accordance with the words of the Rambam: "It is the universal custom to awaken at night in these ten days [of repentance] and to pray in the synagogues words of supplication until the day breaks" (*Hilkhot Teshuvah* 3:4).

For this reason, the evening service, *Ma'ariv*, is abbreviated.[2] The recitation of *Shemoneh Esrei* at night is considered

---

[1] According to the Rav, the contemporary custom of reciting *Seliḥot* in the morning has no halakhic precedent.

[2] In contrast to the *berakhot* associated with *Keriat Shema* in the morning (e.g. אלקי עולם ברחמיך הרבים רחם עלינו), there is virtually no petition at night. Although the *Shaḥarit* prayer of אהבה רבה contains requests for peace and for the ingathering of exiles, אהבת עולם of

reshut (optional), not *ḥovah* (mandatory) (*Berakhot* 27b), because night is the time period in which man's self confidence wanes, when he realizes that he is a lonely creature, physiologically weaker than the animals. He realizes that all his wisdom, discoveries, and technological advances achieved during the day in fact help him very little. Only God can save him. For this reason, *Seliḥot* constitutes *tefillah balaylah,* prayer of night.

The Gemara in *Berakhot* (31a) makes the following statement: "Can a person pray the entire day? It was already explained through Daniel that [prayer is limited to] three times [daily]." Man has no right to offer prayer more than three times a day,[3] and the only sanctioned format for these prayers is the *Shemoneh Esrei.* As an example, if one wishes to pray on behalf of someone who is ill, he either offers a prayer in the framework of *Shemoneh Esrei* such as within the *Refa'einu* ("Heal us") or *Shema Koleinu* ("Hear our voice") paragraphs, or alternatively recites Psalms. There is no specific prayer to be recited for a sick person; we may choose to recite those Psalms that include references to sickness and to God's healing power, but never do we recite a separate prayer.

The reason for the lack of alternate prayer formats outside of *Shemoneh Esrei* is that the very institution of prayer is enigmatic. How can man possibly approach God, knocking on His door, as it were? Who is man to appear before the Universal King and list his petty, insignificant needs? Prayer is indeed a

---

Ma'ariv contains no similar pleas. (ואהבתך אל תסיר ממנו לעולמים) is not a petition but a statement of confidence that God will not forsake the Jewish people; many texts contain the wording לאתסור rather than אלתסיר).
[3] Shmuel did say מתפלל אדם תפילת נדבה, indicating that Shmuel in fact disagreed with this principle: If one so desires, he can indeed recite an additional *Shemoneh Esrei.* Although *Rishonim* accepted Shmuel's view, they added the proviso: אלא אינו נוהגים כך.

special privilege granted to man, but a privilege limited to three times a day. The introduction to the *Shemoneh Esrei*, where we refer to Hashem as "the God of Abraham, the God of Isaac, and the God of Jacob," suggests this motif: were it not for the forefathers establishing the precedent for prayer, we could never display the audacity to approach Him in this way.[ii]

The Rav expanded on this theme in an essay entitled "Ideas Regarding Prayer"[4]:

> Therefore the halakhah insisted on the formal structure of prayer, on its wording and format, and prohibited any laxity regarding the approach of man to God. Without the scriptural references to prayer, it would have been impossible to engage in it...There is no permission for an individual within Israel to add to the three prayers that were established through the scribes of Israel and the sages. We have no permission to compose new prayers. Thus the halakhah establishes in the Talmud: "Rabbi Yehudah said in the name of Shmuel: If one was praying and remembered that he already prayed, he must stop even in the middle [of his prayer]" (*Berakhot* 21a).

In earlier generations, *Seliḥot* on public fast days were said within *Shemoneh Esrei*. Later, they were transferred to the end of *Shemoneh Esrei*, but *Seliḥot* were still integrated into the morning prayer immediately at the conclusion of *Shemoneh Esrei*. Therefore *Seliḥot* never constituted a separate service, with one notable exception: the *Seliḥot* of the *Yamim Nora'im*, the High Holy Days. This special assembly was called *ma'amad ritzui*, a convocation of reconciliation between man and God.

Although *Seliḥot* is a special and separate prayer convocation, it still must fit within the overall format of the other prayers. As a result, one starts the *Seliḥot* service with the *Ashrei* psalms and commences with the half-Kaddish, similar to

---

4 רעיונות על התפלה" באיש ההלכה-גלוי ונסתר" - (*A.L. translation*)

the *Minḥah* (afternoon) prayer. One then recites the prayer *Shome'a Tefillah,*[5] "Hearer of prayer." The function of *Shome'a Tefillah* as an introduction to *Seliḥot* is based on the following passage in Tractate *Berakhot*: "A person should first praise the Holy One Blessed Be He and then pray" (*Berakhot* 32b). Prior to making requests of Hashem one must first glorify Him.[6] In accord with this Talmudic directive, *Shemoneh Esrei* begins with praise of God. In the words of the Rav:

> When a Jew prays, he must be very careful regarding the order of prayer and its form. One does not open with supplication, but rather with words of praise and song, and only then slowly transition to request one's needs. It is supreme arrogance to request of the Holy One Blessed Be He to listen to our requests before we approach Him with praise.[7]

Because *Seliḥot* must also follow the *tefillah* format, *Shome'a Tefillah* performs this same introductory function. The theme of *Shome'a Tefillah* is proclamation and praise of God as the King of the cosmos as well as of Israel. Reciting *Shome'a*

---

[5] The Rav said that although this prayer consists of a wide variety of verses from the Prophets and the Psalms, there is a continuity so natural and a transition so smooth from verse to verse that one could think that they all originated from the same Biblical chapter.

[6] The *Shemoneh Esrei* prayer is organized in the same way, with Hashem's praise serving as an introduction to the subsequent blessings in which our various requests are formulated. On normal fast days, when *Seliḥot* are recited after *Shemoneh Esrei*, the *Shome'a Tefillah* introduction is not said, because the requisite introduction of Hashem's praise was already provided in the *Shemoneh Esrei* repetition.

[7] רעיונות על התפילה, ibid.

Tefillah thus renders the recitation of *Seliḥot* permissible.[8] Only after reciting this collection of verses do we reach the body of the *Seliḥot*, containing as its core the Thirteen Attributes of Mercy. The *Seliḥot* conclude with the full Kaddish: the only example in the liturgy that one says such a Kaddish outside the context of *Shemoneh Esrei*.[iii]

Aside from the regular mitzvah of prayer throughout the year, the plea for forgiveness which is a central feature of the *Seliḥot* supplications is an urgent imperative during the *Yamim Nora'im*.

Teshuvah basically consists of three elements: regret, resolve, and prayer. Regret for past mistakes and a commitment to change one's way of life, as difficult as it may be, is not sufficient. One must also plead with God for forgiveness, for absolution, for atonement. When one commits a sin, he is not only in violation of a precept: he violates his own personality, he loses inspiration, removing himself from the presence of God. Only through prayer can he restore himself.

The first *teshuvah* assembly took place after the incident with the Golden Calf: "And Moses pleaded before God...." The request for forgiveness was an integral part of the confession of the *Kohen Gadol*: "Please, through Your Name, forgive Your nation Israel...."(*Mishnah Yoma* 6:2) The entire 51st Psalm was composed by King David to beg forgiveness and to be cleansed of the sin he committed with Batsheva. Reflecting this emphasis, the Rambam in *Hilkhot Teshuvah* (2:4) states that "among the paths of *teshuvah* is for the returnee to constantly cry out before Hashem in tears and supplication."[iv]

---

[8] The Rav said that because *Shome'a Tefillah* is omitted it was his custom not to recite *Seliḥot* on the morning of Erev Yom Kippur. This

THE *SELIḤOT* PRAYER LEADER

The *Seliḥot* institution itself is based on a remarkable
passage in Tractate *Rosh Hashanah* 17b:

> *Vaya'avor Hashem al panav* -- Rabbi Yoḥanan said: Were it
> not that this was written in Scripture, it would have been
> impossible to suggest it. We learn [from this phrase] that the
> Holy One Blessed Be He wrapped himself like someone who
> leads the prayer services [lit. as an emissary of the con-
> gregation or *sheliaḥ tzibur*] and demonstrated the prayer
> service to Moses, and said to him, "Every time that Israel
> sins, let them perform this service and I will pardon them."

Moses had just successfully entreated God to grant Israel
forgiveness for the sin of the Golden Calf on the very first Yom
Kippur. Hashem's forgiveness was manifest as the statement of
the Thirteen Attributes of Mercy. As a prelude to this statement,
the verse states, *Vaya'avor Hashem al panav,* which is generally
understood to mean that Hashem "passed before his [i.e.
Moses'] face" (Exodus 34:6) prior to stating the Thirteen
Attributes. Rabbi Yoḥanan, however, interpreted the phrase in
an entirely different manner, in the sense that the pronoun "His"
refers to Hashem himself. In the Hebrew idiom, Hashem
"passed by" or covered His own "face," as it were, in the same
manner that a *ḥazan* covers himself with a *talit* during prayer as
he leads the service.

Aside from the astounding imagery of this passage, the
phrase, "Were it not that this was written in Scripture, it would
have been impossible to suggest it," prompts the introduction of
two new halakhic concepts that would otherwise have been
impossible to propose without such explicit textual support.

---

custom is held by many ḥasidim as well.

The first concept involves the introduction of an entirely new prayer service. As mentioned above, it is normally only in the context of *Shemoneh Esrei* that we are allowed to pray at all. The approach to the infinite, absolute sovereign God engendered by prayer is a brazen act, and only through specific halakhic authorization does prayer have legitimacy.

Yet, according to Rabbi Yoḥanan, Hashem is now giving sanction to an entirely new prayer format called *Seliḥot,* separate from the previously instituted *Shemoneh Esrei.* Because establishing a new prayer service would otherwise be prohibited, an explicit scriptural source is needed to sanction its recitation. The Thirteen Attributes of Mercy therefore form the backbone of this new service.

The second concept appropriates a unique role to the *Seliḥot* prayer leader (the *sheliaḥ tzibur*). The entire focus of the *Seliḥot* service rests on this individual. As one example, only he dons the *talit*[9] during the recitation of *Seliḥot*. The reason is that the *sheliaḥ tzibur* represents Hashem, as it were, by playing the same role that Hashem played on that first Yom Kippur on Mount Sinai -- "Were it not that this was written in Scripture, it would have been impossible to suggest it."

As an emissary of the congregation, the *sheliaḥ tzibur* recites the Thirteen Attributes of Mercy in the context of a request that He forgive His people. What is the function of the recitation in his role as Hashem's representative? The often repeated introduction to the Thirteen Attributes in *Seliḥot* includes the phrase *vederekh teshuvah horeita*--"You have pointed the way towards repentance." In the latter context, the

---

[9] During the period of the *Rishonim,* on the evening of Yom Kippur, only the *sheliaḥ tzibur* donned the *talit* as well. The custom for the entire congregation to wear *talitot* was instituted around the time of the Maharal.

recitation of the Thirteen Attributes is an imperative for the congregation to engage in *teshuvah.*

An important detail in Rabbi Yoḥanan's description is that "...the Holy One Blessed Be He wrapped Himself." The purpose of this wrapping, or *atifah,* was for Hashem to hide His face from Moses because Moses would otherwise be consumed by the Divine Presence -- "for man cannot see Me and live" (Exodus 33:20). As a result, in a reenactment of the first Yom Kippur on Mount Sinai, the *sheliaḥ tzibur* engages in *atifah* as well.

A similar halakhah is operative during the blessing of the *Kohanim*: they must be enwrapped within their *talitot* because the Divine Presence rests between their fingers during the blessing (*Sotah* 38a *Rashi s.v. Uv'mikdash).*[v] The Rambam noted an apparent anomaly in this scene when he stated:

> And don't wonder to yourself and say, "How can the blessing of this ordinary person be effective," for the acceptance of the blessing is not dependent on the *Kohanim,* but on the Holy One Blessed Be He, as the verse states, "And they will place My Name on the Children of Israel and I will bless them." The *kohanim* perform what they were commanded, and the Holy One Blessed Be He in His mercy blesses Israel in accordance with His desire" (*Hilkhot Tefillah U'nesi'at Kapayim* 15:7).

In a similar vein, the following passage from the *Mishneh Torah* touches on the same theme:

> What is honor [*kibud*]? This is what our sages said, that it is a mitzvah to wash one's face, hands, and feet in hot water on Erev Shabbat due to the honor of Shabbat, and he wraps himself in a *talit* and sits with his head covered, anxiously awaiting the reception of Shabbat as if he were to go out to greet a king, and the early sages would gather their students on the eve of the Sabbath and wrap themselves and say: "Come let us greet the Sabbath King" (*Hilkhot Shabbat* 30:2).

Greeting the Sabbath *(Kabbalat Shabbat)* required enwrapping oneself, because *Kabbalat Shabbat* is equivalent to greeting the Divine Presence.[10]

Since it is only the *sheliaḥ tzibur* who is enwrapped in the *talit*, it is he that is responsible for the consciousness that one stands directly *lifnei Hashem*, before Hashem, during the *Yamim Nora'im*. The *Shekhinah* rests on him.

---

[10] This concept forms the entire basis for the *Kabbalat Shabbat* service. See, for example, the כגוונא passage recited in the *Nusaḥ Sefard* liturgy.

NOTES

ⁱ In a 1970 lecture in Boston, the Rav explained that the thematic tension of man as both exalted and lowly finds specific expression in the Yom Kippur liturgy. The aggrandizement of man is the theme of the *piyyutim* of *Shaḥarit*: אמרו לאלוקים,אשר אומץ תהלתך, על ישראל גאותו. This motif culminates in the *Kedushah* -- כתר יתנו לך, where man, rising to the level of the angels, crowns the Lord. However, towards the end of the *Amidah* repetition, the *Seliḥot* theme of the worthlessness, defilement, and degradation of man appears, culminating in the recitation of the *vidui*. The Rav also noted that these two themes are strikingly juxtaposed in the *Ne'ilah* prayer:

...ומותר האדם מן הבהמה אין כי הכל הבל-- אתה הבדלת אנוש מראש ותכירהו
לעמוד לפניך...

ⁱⁱ The Gemara (*Berakhot* 4b) states: "[for] all who say [*Ashrei*] three times a day it is promised that [they merit] the World to Come." In a lecture given on October 6, 1976, the Rav explained the importance of the *Ashrei* psalm in light of this discussion. The first part of *Ashrei*, with the Rav's clarification in brackets, is as follows:

> I will exalt You, my God the King, and I will bless Your Name forever. All day I will bless You, and I will praise Your Name forever. [But how is this possible?] God is infinite and exalted [above all prayer], and His greatness has no limit! [What right do I have with my limited vocabulary to undertake to praise Him? Isn't this arrogant and impudent? Yet,] Generation to generation [before me] praised Your works, and Your might and omnipotence they have passed on to others. [Therefore, I also deserve to describe] the beauty of Your Glory, and Your wonders I will relate.

This concept is the meaning behind the maxim תפלות אבות תקנום
(ברכות כו:) -- the very concept of prayer was legitimized by our
forefathers.

iii In his 1980 *Teshuvah Derashah*, the Rav emphasized another
fundamental difference between prayer and *Seliḥot*. The basic building
block of prayer within *Shemoneh Esrei* is the *berakhah*, while in
Seliḥot, the basic unit is the Biblical verse. Because the *berakhah* as
such is of Rabbinical origin, the *Shemoneh Esrei* is in reality *Torah
Sheb'al Peh*, while *Seliḥot* is *Torah Shebikhtav*.

iv The significance of *Seliḥot* as *tze'akah* is a theme that the Rav
expands in the essay "Redemption, Prayer and Talmud Torah",
Tradition (June 1978):

> What is the structure of liberation through prayer? We find, upon
> analysis, that the process of redemption of the individual and the
> community through prayer is similar to the redemption from Egypt,
> as described by the Zohar. There are three stages. 1) No prayer at all
> - the silence of atrophy, the absence of a need-awareness; 2) An
> outcry, a voice, saturated with suffering and sadness; 3) The birth of
> the word, i.e., the birth of prayer through the word.
>
> It is in this second stage, with the awakening of the need-
> awareness, that prayer makes its entry. The level of intermediate
> prayer is not yet תפלה but צעקה, a human outcry...There is as yet no
> word, no sentence; although the emotional awareness has awakened,
> the logos of need is still dormant, silent. There is not yet a clear
> understanding of what one is crying for. There is distress and loud
> human weeping. צעקה is primordial prayer, the voice restored, the
> word still lacking...
>
> In halachic liturgy, prayer at the stage of צעקה is called סליחות.
> There are four distinctive characteristics of סליחות: 1) recital of the
> Thirteen Attributes of Mercy (י"ג מדות); 2) confession (וידוי); 3)
> repetition of short sentences distinguished by simplicity of form
> (e.g. מי שענה לאברהם...הוא יעננו); 4) reading of prophetic verses of
> petition or praise.

However, at this point, the Rav comes to an apparently different conclusion regarding *Seliḥot* than what is laid out in his *derashah* here:

> The main distinction between תפלה (represented by the עמידה) and צעקה consists in the absence of strict formulation in the case of סליחות. Prayer as צעקה lacks the gradual development of theme, the structural formalism, and the etiquette-like orderliness which halakhah required of the מתפלל, the prayerful person.

Here the Rav seems to discount the fundamental importance of, for example, the שומע תפלה introduction, or the full Kaddish at the conclusion of *Seliḥot*. The סליחות-צעקה equation thus contrasts with the Rav's emphasis in this *derashah* on the importance of form in *Seliḥot* as an alternate prayer format.

^v The Rav expands on this point in *On Repentance*, "Repentance and Free Choice":

> The eternal love of the Creator of the World emanates through the personality of the *kohen*: "the *Shekhinah* dwells between his fingertips." Why does the Talmud specify fingertips? Why not from his forehead, his head, his face? In the case of Moses our teacher, the *Shekhinah* emanated its rays of glory from his face. Why, then, in the case of the *Kohanim* does it vibrate from between their fingertips? Perhaps because the fingertips represent man's self-seeking, his tendency to take things and hold onto them. The hand is aggressive: if it grabs hold of something, it does not release it. "Close not your fist to your impoverished brother," we have been commanded. The fingers represent man's possessiveness, his attempt to hold onto assets, occasionally also onto those which are not his. During the priestly blessing, these fingers of the hand are spread apart, extended, as though to proclaim that the moment a *kohen* ascends the pulpit, the usual way of the world in which we too often witness violation of the commandment, "Harden not your heart and close not your fist against your impoverished brother," is transformed and recedes. Its place is taken by love, by care for a friend, by open fingers eager to serve as a channel for the transmission of the grace of the Almighty to all His creatures from

here to eternity. As it is written: "And they shall set My Name upon the Children of Israel and I will bless them" (Numbers 6:27). Anyone who encounters such love of humanity, such goodness of heart, such devotion to others - and fails to see in this the reflection of the glory of God, then his soul is dull, like that of the person who sees a beautiful rainbow yet fails to recognize in it the splendor of the *Shekhinah*.

The Approach and Arrival
of Yom Kippur[*]

A theme that the Rav consistently discussed in his *teshuvah derashot* is the gap between the intellectual and the emotional realms among contemporary Orthodoxy.[i] In his 1976 *teshuvah derashah*, the Rav phrased the problem in this way:

> *My religious world-view was formed not only through learning Torah, but also by my religious experience...I continually refer to the two traditions of Torah learning -- halakhah and that of religious life and feeling -- the enthusiasm, the love of Hashem, the yearning for Hashem... The first is relatively easy to impart; I can give long lectures on shofar, the halakhot of* teshuvah, *the* Avodah, *etc. with great depth and thoroughness. Yet*

[*] BASED ON THE 1976, 1978, and 1980 *TESHUVAH DERASHOT*

what is easy for me [to explain] regarding the first tradition is very difficult regarding the second tradition.

To recount what Jews of earlier generations-- not only the Gedolei Yisrael *but Jews in general -- experienced on the* Yamim Nora'im *-- the yearning, the nostalgia that overtook one's entire being -- to impart the emotion is almost impossible. As a child, I remember how infectious that emotion was: I felt the same yearning as everyone else without really understanding what exactly I was yearning for. Those emotions which overtook me as a child stimulate me still today, and my whole* Weltanschauung, *my whole religious philosophy, is a result of this experience.*

Contemporary Orthodoxy is well grounded intellectually. In spite of this, however, its followers lack passion and enthusiasm. This deficiency is especially evident on Rosh Hashanah and Yom Kippur...

How can a Jew pray on Yom Kippur and not feel the greatness, the fire and holiness of this day? How can I possibly impart such an experience? Perhaps one can begin to awaken the ecstatic feeling by discussing the customs and laws which we observe on Yom Kippur. From within the allegedly dry confines of Jewish law, there is an awesome, warm, enormous world -- there is a definite transition from Halakhah to service of Hashem. Perhaps through such a discussion, the audience will be awakened to the religious mood that a Jew must find himself in on Yom Kippur.

The Rav indicated that the powerful religious experience was actually felt the day before Yom Kippur as well:

I remember how difficult it was to go to sleep on Erev Yom Kippur. The shoḥet *(ritual slaughterer) used to come at the break of dawn to provide chickens for the* kaparos *ritual, and later the people would give charity. The wallets of Jews were open twice a year, Erev Yom Kippur and Purim -- but especially on Erev Yom Kippur. Minḥah, vidui, the final meal before the fast* [seudah hamafsekes], *my grandfather's preparations -- all made Erev Yom Kippur a special entity, not only halakhic, but emotional and religious as well.*[ii]

Erev Yom Kippur constitutes the herald that the Ribono Shel Olam *is coming, that* lifnei Hashem tit'haru" -- *"before Hashem you shall be purified."*

The Rav expressed the hope that perhaps through the discussion of the halakhic status and significance of Erev Yom Kippur, the audience could begin to appreciate the intense emotional feeling to which he was referring. Instead of a gulf, there is a definite nexus from halakhic legalism to emotional experience.

THE HALAKHIC STATUS OF EREV YOM KIPPUR

Erev Yom Kippur performs the function of informing us that we are about to encounter the *Ribono Shel Olam*. The day therefore has a special status in halakhah. A Gemara in *Yoma* introduces the halakhic framework for understanding the unique nature of Erev Yom Kippur:

Ḥiya Bar Rav from Difti stated in a *baraita:* "And you shall afflict your souls on the ninth [of Tishrei]..." Does one fast on the ninth? Does one not fast on the tenth? Rather, the verse states that anyone who eats and drinks on the ninth, it is considered as if he fasted on [both] the ninth and tenth" (*Yoma* 81b).

The concept introduced in this halakhah is that the mitzvah to eat and drink on the ninth day of Tishrei is not a fulfillment of a mitzvah that pertains to the ninth per se, but rather an obligation that actually involves the day of Yom Kippur, the tenth day of Tishrei. Erev Yom Kippur is appended to Yom Kippur in order to fulfill certain specific obligations which would otherwise be precluded due to the various prohibitions of Yom Kippur.

Yom Kippur carries the obligations inherent in its status as a festival or *Yom Tov*. Although the most obvious manifestation of this status is the prohibition of work, *Yom Tov* carries with it other obligations as well. To such obligations are *kibud* and *oneg*, based on a Talmudic explanation of the verse: "If you turn away your foot from the Shabbat, from pursuing your business on My holy day, and call Shabbat a delight (*oneg*), and [call] the holy day of Hashem honorable (*mekhubad*)..." (Isaiah 58:13). Although this verse refers specifically to Shabbat, the *kibud* and *oneg* obligations pertain to *Yom Tov* as well.

The Mitzvah of *Kibud*

The Rambam states the following in regard to the mitzvah of *kibud:*

> What is honor *[kibud]*? This that our sages said, that it is a mitzvah to wash one's face, hands, and feet in hot water on Erev Shabbat due to the honor of Shabbat, and he wraps himself in a *talit* and sits with his head covered, anxiously awaiting *[yiḥol]* the reception of Shabbat as if he were going to greet a king... (*Hilkhot Shabbat* 30:2).

Kibud is manifested in the obligation to wear special clothes in honor of the day, as well as to clean and decorate the house in order to increase the festivity, in accordance with a passage in the Gemara:

> The Exilarch asked Rav Hamnuna: "Why does the verse state, 'And [call] the Holy of Hashem honorable'? [Rav Hamnuna] answered, ['The Holy of Hashem'] refers to Yom Kippur, in which there is no eating and no drinking; one must honor the day by donning fresh clothing" (*Shabbat* 119a).

The above passage presents a difficulty to the Me'iri. There is no reason to think that Yom Kippur does not carry the same obligation as Shabbat or any other festival (*Mishneh Torah, Hilkhot Yom Tov* 6:16) regarding the mitzvah of *kibud*. Why then, according to Rav Hamnuna, must the Torah go out of its way to emphasize that *kibud* is specifically applicable on Yom Kippur?

The Me'iri answers that the renewed emphasis of Rav Hamnuna regarding *kibud* on Yom Kippur suggests that the *kibud* imperative on Yom Kippur is even greater than it is on Shabbat. The honor that one accords Yom Kippur should be double that of a normal Shabbat: one must wear his absolute best clothes on Yom Kippur.

The Rav expanded on the Me'iri's point. Yom Kippur possesses two aspects of Shabbat, as implied in the Biblical appellation *Shabbat Shabbaton. Shabbat* refers to the injunction to withdraw from work, while *Shabbaton* refers to withdrawal from eating. The magnified *kibud* obligation on Yom Kippur reflects this duality, a double Sabbath that engenders a double *kibud*.

In contrast to the preparation for Shabbat, when simply "washing one's face, hands, and feet" is sufficient, the augmented *kibud* for Yom Kippur is expressed by total immersion in a mikveh. On Shabbat the purpose of the washing is to remove dirt, so that one enters Shabbat in a state of physical cleanliness. On Yom Kippur, the purpose of the immersion in a mikveh goes beyond simple cleanliness; the intent is to achieve spiritual purity.[1] The immersion takes place prior to the beginning of Yom Kippur because the anticipation is such that he simply cannot wait until Yom Kippur itself to achieve purity.

The word *yiḥol* as used by the Rambam therefore suggests a nervous tension, a yearning, a panting expectancy, as we prepare for our encounter with God on Yom Kippur. One waits with breathless anticipation for Yom Kippur to arrive. One yearns impatiently, as if continually running to a window, excitedly counting the minutes before Hashem's arrival.

The Mitzvah of *Oneg*

Oneg, another obligation mentioned in the verse in Isaiah pertaining to Shabbat and Yom Tov, is described by the Rambam as follows:

> What is *oneg*? This is what our sages said, that it is necessary to prepare cooked, delicious delicacies and spiced drinks for Shabbat, all based on a person's means, and the more one extends himself through the preparation of many different delicious foods the more he is praiseworthy (*Hilkhot Shabbat* 30:7).

The mitzvah of *oneg* specifically involves eating. Therefore the obligation of *oneg* on Yom Kippur, a fast day, is problematic. As a result, many *Rishonim* maintain that the obligation of *oneg* is necessarily suspended on Yom Kippur, based on a close reading of the passage in the Gemara: "The Exilarch asked Rav Hamnuna: 'Why does the verse state, "and

---

[1] The Vilna Gaon quoting the Mordekhai states this idea explicitly: the purpose of immersion in a mikveh prior to Yom Kippur is not necessarily to remove any specific impurity, but rather because of the injunction of "before Hashem you shall be purified."

to the Holy of Hashem it is honored"?' [Rav Hamnuna] answered ['it'] refers to Yom Kippur, in which there is no eating and no drinking" (*Shabbat* 119a). The inclusion of *kibud* and the omission of the *oneg* concept in this Talmudic passage would imply that Yom Kippur indeed contains no aspect of *oneg*.

Yet, there is no explicit Talmudic reference indicating that the obligation of *oneg* does not apply on Yom Kippur. Consequently, the Rav posits a role for *oneg* within the Yom Kippur imperative based on a close reading of the Rambam: "...it is necessary to prepare cooked, delicious delicacies...and the more one extends himself through the preparation of many different delicious foods the more he is praiseworthy" (*Hilkhot Shabbat* 30:7). The objective of the mitzvah of *oneg* is preparation. A similar theme of preparation on the day before Yom Kippur is discussed in the following passage from a Rashi in Gemara *Yoma* 81b:

> *"Anyone who eats and drinks.."*.-- This is what the verse implies: "And you shall afflict your soul on the ninth," meaning prepare yourself on the ninth so that you can fast on the tenth.

On Shabbat, the mitzvah of *oneg* consists of preparing food in order to eat properly. On Yom Kippur, the mitzvah of *oneg* consists of eating and drinking in order to prepare oneself to fast properly. According to the Rav, *oneg* is an imperative that applies to Yom Kippur as well as Shabbat.

Through a close reading of Ḥiya Bar Difti's statement in the Gemara in *Yoma,* the Rav further buttresses the contention that the *oneg* obligation of Yom Kippur is, in fact, fulfilled on the previous day. Ḥiya Bar Difti states: "...Anyone who eats and drinks on the ninth, it is considered as if he fasted on the ninth and tenth." This passage implies that the mitzvah of eating on the day before Yom Kippur is not intrinsic to the ninth of

Tishrei. Through the act of eating on the ninth of Tishrei one is credited with an extension of an obligation pertaining to Yom Kippur itself. The status of Yom Kippur as a *Yom Tov* includes an obligation to eat. Since we cannot eat on Yom Kippur itself, we do so on the previous day. Eating on the day before Yom Kippur is therefore not the consumption we experience on a weekday, but rather the feast of a *Yom Tov*.

Erev Yom Kippur thus has a special halakhic status[2] that transcends that of a simple weekday. One eats on Erev Yom Kippur, and through this preparation for the fast the obligatory *oneg* aspect is fulfilled. In this way, Erev Yom Kippur reflects the holiness of Yom Kippur itself.

The *Vidui* of Erev Yom Kippur

A compelling proof of the special halakhic status of Erev Yom Kippur can be found in a Gemara in Yoma: "The Rabbis taught: There is a mitzvah of *vidui* on Erev Yom Kippur at nightfall. However, the sages stated that he must say *vidui* before he eats in case he gets drunk during his meal" (*Yoma* 87b).

This passage thus indicates that there is a Rabbinic obligation ("the sages stated") to recite *vidui* during the *Minḥah* service, prior to the final meal before the fast (the *seudah hamafseket*).

There are a number of significant differences between this passage in the Gemara and the Rambam in their respective descriptions of the mitzvah of *vidui* on Erev Yom Kippur. The Rambam states the following in *Hilkhot Teshuvah*:

> Yom Kippur is the time of repentance for all, for individuals and for the many, and it is the culmination of forgiveness and

---

[2] The Rav used a term with specific halakhic implications: חלות שם

pardon for Israel. Therefore all are obligated to do *teshuvah* and confess on Yom Kippur. And the mitzvah of *vidui* on Yom Kippur starts while it is still daytime before one eats, in case one chokes on his meal [and expires] before having confessed (*Hilkhot Teshuvah* 2:7).

The most obvious difference between the Gemara and the Rambam is that the Rambam implies that the mitzvah of *vidui* on Erev Yom Kippur is Biblical in origin,[3] while the Gemara explicitly states that the mitzvah is of Rabbinic origin. This discrepancy seems so irreconcilable that the Rav goes so far as to suggest that the Rambam's halakhah is based on a variant wording in the Gemara -- wording which omitted any mention of the mitzvah's Rabbinic origin.

However, even if one were to emend the text of the Gemara to match the opinion of the Rambam, the latter would still be difficult to fathom. The standard version of the Gemara states that the reason for the obligation of *vidui* on Erev Yom Kippur is because the person may get drunk and not be able to recite *vidui* in Ma'ariv. In order to avoid this possibility, we compel him to say *vidui* at *Minhah* instead.

The Rambam, using a differing text *(girsa)* of the Gemara, gives an alternative rationale for the *Minhah vidui*: perhaps the person will choke on his *se'udah hamafseket* and expire. This explanation presents a major difficulty. If someone dies before the onset of Yom Kippur, he would presumably not experience the atonement that the day of Yom Kippur itself imparts, unlike

---

[3] The implication derives from the fact that the Rambam makes no distinction between the Biblical obligation to "do *teshuvah* and confess on Yom Kippur" and the time that this obligation actually takes place, "on Yom Kippur...while it is still daytime." If, according to the Rambam, *vidui* on Erev Yom Kippur were indeed Rabbinic in origin, the Rambam would have explicitly said, "But the Rabbis state that the mitzvah of *vidui* on Yom Kippur starts while it is still daytime...."

someone who is intoxicated but nonetheless alive. What possible function could the *vidui* of *Minḥah* therefore serve according to the Rambam?

The conclusion that must inevitably be drawn is that Erev Yom Kippur is appended to the day of Yom Kippur itself in respect to the holiness of the day (*kedushat hayom*). The person who chokes on the final meal leaves the world, but with the atonement afforded by Yom Kippur, having already said the requisite *vidui* in the preceding Minḥah service. Thus the *vidui* of Erev Yom Kippur, coupled with the holiness of the day of Yom Kippur, provides the necessary atonement,[iii] since this holiness actually commences on Erev Yom Kippur.

The conclusion that we therefore reach is that in both the aspects of *oneg* and *vidui*, Erev Yom Kippur is an extension of, and is identified with, Yom Kippur itself.

That Erev Yom Kippur plays such a role is implied in the verse, "For through this day He will atone for you, to purify you; from all your sins before Hashem you shall be purified" (Leviticus 16:30). According to the Ramban (Naḥmanides), the word "before" signifies a point in time rather than a point in space. Thus, the Ramban explains the phrase "before Hashem you shall be purified" in the sense that before one enters Yom Kippur, he must be pure.[iv] As a result, the Ramban maintains that the main *vidui* of Yom Kippur is a confession that one says after sunset but before nightfall (Ramban, *Yoma* 87b).[v] In contrast, the Rambam is of the opinion that *vidui* after sunset is too late to fulfill the imperative of attaining purity prior to Yom Kippur. This *vidui* of purification must be recited on Erev Yom Kippur.

It is therefore clear that on Erev Yom Kippur there are two aspects of preparation; the physical preparation, consisting of eating and drinking through which one fulfills the *oneg* obligation; and the spiritual preparation, in order to be spiritually ready to stand pure before Hashem on Yom Kippur (i.e. as a *tahor*).

Proper preparation is, in fact, a necessary condition for any encounter with holiness. As one example, in the three-day prelude to receiving the Torah, Moses warned the nation "Be ready for the third day; do not approach a woman" (Exodus 19:15). Similarly, Aaron had to submit to a seven-day preparation period prior to the dedication of the Tabernacle, and every *Kohen Gadol* subsequently went through a similar sequester prior to Yom Kippur. What is the analogy between Aaron's preparation period prior to the Tabernacle dedication and Yom Kippur? Both involved an encounter with holiness. Holiness does not arrive suddenly; it comes only by the invitation inherent in the act of preparation. Erev Yom Kippur thus becomes the day on which we prepare ourselves for the awesome experience of "before Hashem you shall be purified."

Immersion and Sprinkling

To clarify the respective roles of the *vidui* of Erev Yom Kippur versus the *vidui* of Yom Kippur itself, the Rav quoted from the homily of Rabbi Akiva at the end of Tractate *Yoma* (8:9):

> Rabbi Akiva said: Happy are you, O Israel. Before whom are you purified and who purifies you? Your Father in Heaven, as it is stated: "And I will sprinkle on you purifying waters and you shall be cleansed," and it states: "Hashem is the hope [*mikveh*] of Israel": just as a *mikveh* purifies the impure, so does the Holy One Blessed Be He purify Israel.

Rabbi Akiva implies that there are two types of purification from sin: one involving sprinkling (*haza'ah*), and a second involving immersion (*tevilah*) in a mikveh.

Haza'ah requires the involvement of a second person to perform the sprinkling: "And a pure man shall sprinkle upon the impure" (Numbers 19:19). One cannot perform the sprinkling ritual on himself. In *tevilah*, unlike *haza'ah*, there is no second party involvement. The entire initiative rests with the individual who desires purification.

Parallel to these two types of purification are two types of *teshuvah*. There are individuals who, through their own initiative, decide that they no longer wish to be sinners. This is the type of *teshuvah* that is operative throughout the year through Erev Yom Kippur. In the words of the liturgist: Hashem "waits for the evil person, and desires his becoming righteous" (from the liturgical poem *Vekhol Ma'aminim*) and, "Until the day he dies You wait for him -- and if he returns You will immediately receive Him" (from *U'netaneh Tokef*).

But there is yet another type of *teshuvah*. In this type Hashem Himself helps the person to repent, as stated in the *Amidah* of *Ne'ilah*: "You offer a hand to sinners, and Your right hand is outstretched to receive those who repent." Hashem Himself cleanses man, he teaches him of the degradation of sin and the beauty of *teshuvah*. Fallen man finds an outstretched hand to help him. Hashem plays an active role and personally accompanies man to the gates of repentance.

Teshuvah and *vidui* are effective all year round, because Hashem "waits for the evil person, and desires his becoming righteous." The objective of every public fast day throughout the year is to inspire *teshuvah*. Similarly, on Erev Yom Kippur, Hashem is the "Mikveh of Israel," and He waits patiently for our *teshuvah*. The Rambam calls the mikveh waters *mei hada'at* -- the waters of knowledge (*Hilkhot Mikvaot* 11:12), because *teshuvah* requires recognition of sin. The other requisite steps of *teshuvah*, remorse and resolve not to continue sinning, both stem from this recognition, from this knowledge. The sinner has in a real sense lost his prestige. This lost sense of self-worth is restored by immersion in the mikveh.

In contrast, on Yom Kippur itself, with the power of the day of Yom Kippur to effect purity, Hashem takes the sinner by the hand, as it were, and leads him to Him. "And I will sprinkle on you purifying waters and you shall be cleansed."

Tevilah and *haza'ah* actually represent the purification processes for two different types of sinners.

The motivation for sin often stems from external influences. Unethical and sinful acts are done through external pressures and influences. In effect, circumstances force the sinner's hand. It is this type of sinner that addresses God through the *Tefillah Zakkah* meditation recited just prior to Kol Nidrei:

> It is revealed and known before You that I did not intend to perform all [these] sins and iniquities, to provoke You and rebel against You; I merely followed the counsel of the evil inclination which continually spreads a net at my feet to ensnare me. But I am poor and destitute, a worm and not a man. My strength was insufficient to stand up against it, and the burden of supporting my household and the distractions of time and their vicissitudes have befouled me....

The *Hayyei Adam*, the composer of this meditation, here provides an apology for sin. In reality the sin is not intrinsic to the sinner. The sin is a result of external influences -- from the difficulties associated with supporting a family, for example, or through other events not within one's control. These types of sins are extraneous to the personality of the sinner. This sinner is not identified with sin *per se*.

Sin is associated with the act of falling. Upon seeing a patient who has injured himself in a fall, a doctor tries to probe the reason for the fall. Sometimes, one falls simply because he inadvertently trips over some object, while at other times one can fall due to a physiological defect in space perception such as dizziness. Both types of falls can be equally injurious. Yet, if the cause is external, the person is intrinsically healthy. If he has enough strength of character, this type of sinner can free himself from sin by negotiating or removing the obstacles that stand in his way.

However, when the cause of the fall is a result of distorted perception, a different therapy is needed. Similarly, if the sin is a result of a spiritually perplexed personality, if it derives from a fundamentally false *Weltanschauung*, then sin is intrinsic and he cannot do *teshuvah* without outside help. To change the false system of values that results in sin, one must have help from Hashem.[4]

It is very difficult to do *teshuvah* when this means not only desisting from sin, but replacing the very ideology that motivates sin. God's active participation is therefore required. This is the message of Rabbi Akiva: "Before whom are you purified and who purifies you?" The statement is not "who pardons you" or "who provides atonement." Hashem aids in the sinner's purification.

KOL NIDREI

Kol Nidrei as a Reflection of *Teshuvah*

The custom of reciting Kol Nidrei finds its origin in the Gaonic period. This recitation was apparently unknown in the previous generations in Babylonia, and indeed there was a

---

[4] The Rav used this analogy to explain the motivation to sin by the United States as opposed to the then Soviet Union. When America as a country sins through its policy-making, it does so out of external influences, such as when it pressures Israel out of fear of losing its foreign oil sources. In contrast, in the Soviet Union, the hatred for Israel was intrinsic to their ideology.

difference of opinion among Gaonim as to whether or not Kol Nidrei should be instituted as the introduction to the holy day of Yom Kippur.

The reason for its present day popularity is clear. Through the recitation of this formula, all vows are annulled retroactively. As a result, after reciting Kol Nidrei one need not repent for having vowed falsely.

However, an obvious question arises in light of this explanation. If the day of Yom Kippur itself along with repentance atones for all sins, why the necessity for Kol Nidrei at all?

The answer is equally as obvious. If through recitation of Kol Nidrei one can remove a specific type of sin retroactively, one should not have to rely on repentance and Yom Kippur to perform the same function. Because there is no such recourse for sins other than false vows, Yom Kippur and repentance are required to eliminate other transgressions.

Yet, there is another more visceral motivation behind the recitation of Kol Nidrei.

True *teshuvah* is accompanied by a deep sense of humiliation for having sinned in the first place. Ezra the Scribe emphasized the importance of shame in the act of *teshuvah* by stating: "My God, I am embarrassed and ashamed to lift my face to You, My God, for our sins have multiplied above our heads and our sins extend unto heaven" (Ezra 9:6). Reflecting this theme, the Gemara (*Berakhot* 12b) states: "Whoever commits a sin and becomes ashamed because of it, all his sins are forgiven." The Rambam (*Hilkhot Teshuvah* 1:1) echoes this theme in his description of *vidui*: "Please, Hashem, I have sinned and transgressed before You...and now I have remorse and am ashamed of my acts."

Remorse, a major component of repentance, must be accompanied by a sense of shame for the act of sinning. As an example, if one who routinely violates the Sabbath thinks to himself, "I may as well observe Shabbat; I have nothing to lose," the key element of shame is missing, and true repentance is lacking. If, on the other hand, he thinks, "What a fool I am for not keeping Shabbat; I would have had different children, a different household, a different life," the sense of regret is so intense that the sin becomes a source of deep embarrassment. This emotion truly constitutes shame.

The person who experiences shame would desperately welcome any possible opportunity to somehow undo the act which resulted in the humiliation, to turn back the clock so to speak. He cannot tolerate the very thought that he actually indulged in sin. The true penitent is therefore not quite satisfied with atonement per se; he would greatly prefer to extirpate the sin as if it never existed. By reciting Kol Nidrei, we convey this desire and thus attest to our Maker that the remorse we feel for all sins, not just false vows, contains within it the critical element of shame.

There is, however, a second version of Kol Nidrei, and based on the rendition one uses, the function of the formula is fundamentally altered. The form that is most often used states that all vows be annulled "...from the past Yom Kippur until this Yom Kippur...." This version is consistent with the above explanation that Kol Nidrei serves to uproot vows made in the past.

However, in another widely used version, there is a subtle change in wording, where one requests that vows be annulled "...from this Yom Kippur until the next Yom Kippur...." Rabbeinu Tam, who prefers this latter wording,[5] explains that Kol Nidrei is in fact not an annulment of past vows at all, but rather is a conditional statement that future vows uttered throughout the coming year should be annulled.

In light of the latter reading, we must reinterpret the relationship of Kol Nidrei to Yom Kippur. What is the symbolic

---

ספר הישר סימן ק׳ . רא״ש נדרים פ״ג ס״ה. טור או״ח תריט[5]

relevance of Kol Nidrei to the broader themes of Yom Kippur in Rabbeinu Tam's version?

Aside from shame, another critical component in the *teshuvah* process is the resolve not to continue sinning. In detailing the *teshuvah* process, the Rambam is quite strict in this requirement. The resolve must be so sincere that Hashem himself must testify that the penitent will never again engage in such a sin *(Hilkhot Teshuvah*, 2:2). The person must also engage in specific actions to demonstrate this sincerity: "Among the ways of *teshuvah* is for the penitent to call out constantly to Hashem in weeping and supplication, and for him to give charity according to his means, and for him to greatly distance himself from the sin that he committed" *(Hilkhot Teshuvah* 2:4).

No matter how sincere the intention, the penitent must provide some type of guarantee of his resolve through concrete action. In the case of false vows, such a guarantee would take the form of a conditional statement that all vows uttered in the future be voided. Such a statement is the best possible proof that he will never again be guilty of such a sin.

Rabbeinu Tam's version of Kol Nidrei therefore gives expression to our determination not to continue sinning, while the earlier version is symbolic of our deep shame for having sinned in the first place. Whichever version one uses, Kol Nidrei resonates as a clear expression of the proper mood upon the arrival of Yom Kippur. At the same time, recitation of Kol Nidrei sends a message to man that his *teshuvah* must be strict and disciplined, including both key halakhic requirements of remorse and resolve.

Accompanying the Cantor at Kol Nidrei

Reenacting the Battle of Amalek

There is a universal practice that two people stand on either side of the cantor during his recitation of Kol Nidrei.[6] This custom is associated with public fasts in general,[7] based on a passage from *Pirkei Derab Eliezer*. This source quotes a verse in Exodus (see Rashi on Exodus 17:10) describing Moses' entreaty to Hashem during the first encounter of the Israelites with the Amalekite enemy: "And Moses' hands were heavy, and they took a rock and placed it under him and he sat on it, and Aaron and Ḥur supported his hands...and he was with his hands in faith until the setting of the sun" (Exodus 17:12).

Moses' hands, held continually aloft in prayer, were heavy and required support from his brother and nephew to stay elevated. The task of requesting deliverance is too formidable for an individual alone, no matter how great the individual is. Even Moses himself could not approach Hashem on his own to ask Him to rescue the Jewish nation from Amalek; Moses needed two others to demonstrate that his entreaty represented the will of the whole nation.

---

[6] The Rav indicated that the custom in his shul was that two people stood next to the cantor during all of Yom Kippur, although the Magen Avraham suggests that the custom only applies to Kol Nidrei. During the *Avodah* recitation, there is a special obligation for two people to stand next to the *ḥazan*: in Volozhin, on one side stood the Netziv, while on the other side was R. Ḥaim Soloveitchik.

[7] The custom that two stand next to the *ḥazan* during Kol Nidrei is also based on the necessity to form a *beit din* for the purpose of *hatarat nedarim*. However, according to Rabbeinu Tam's version of Kol Nidrei, which does not involve *hatarat nedarim* at all, this reason is not applicable.

The operative Biblical phrase which addresses this issue directly is: "And it will be forgiven to the entire congregation of Israel..." (Numbers 15:26). The forgiveness is granted to Israel as a group, of which an individual has only a part. Israel as a group does not merely *ask* for forgiveness, it *demands* forgiveness.[vi] Through our covenant with God, He is contractually obligated, as it were, to provide forgiveness as part of our membership within greater Israel.

The *Kohen Gadol* on Yom Kippur acted both as an agent of Hashem and as an agent of the people (*Tosafot Yoma* 19b s.v. *mi ikka*). The presence of the two assistants who accompanied the *Kohen Gadol* during most parts of the Yom Kippur service in the Temple demonstrated that the *Kohen Gadol* was not acting on his own, but indeed was sent to represent all Israel.

The incident of Moses as he held up his hands during the battle with Amalek suggests a second motif relevant to Yom Kippur. The Ḥasidim of Ḥabad used to call the night of Rosh Hashanah "Coronation Night." It is the night in which Jews place the crown of sovereignty on Hashem, as it were. It is the night that we refer to Hashem as *HaMelekh HaKadosh*, the Holy King, in the *Amidah* prayer for the first time.

But does Hashem actually accept this crown from us? The concluding verse of the Amalek incident in Exodus provides the answer. "For there is a hand on the throne of God: Hashem maintains a war against Amalek from generation to generation" (Exodus 17:16). The word "throne" and the name "God" are both truncated in this verse, to which Rashi explains: "His Name is not whole and His throne is not whole until the name of Amalek will be eradicated." Hashem's sovereignty is not absolute as long as Amalek continues to exist. Every Rosh Hashanah and Yom Kippur in the *Amidah* we request that Hashem accept the crown that is being offered: "And so too, Hashem our God, instill Your fear upon all Your works...then

You, Hashem, will reign alone..." Yet, tragically, as long as Amalek exists He does not accept it.

Who, then, is Amalek, whose presence somehow inhibits Hashem's sovereignty?

When Hashem created the earth from *tohu vavohu*, chaos and void (Genesis 1:2), He did not replace the chaos entirely. Some of this primordial entropy was allowed to remain, so that man, through his own effort, could strive to eliminate it. Amalek represents this leftover chaos, identified with sin, which remained behind so man himself can actively play a role in destroying it. [vii]

The Jew must eternally battle this insidious enemy, the *tohu vavohu* which resides within each of us. During the Days of Awe, the imperative of the battle is the destruction of sin from within ourselves. Amalek exists within everyone, and through our attempt at his destruction we at the same time endeavor to crown Hashem. Yet, God's sovereignty is inhibited to the extent that we fall short of the total eradication of sin.

Each Yom Kippur is a replica of that first pivotal battle with Amalek, when Aaron and Ḥur supported Moses during his prayer. Evoking this imagery, two elders of the congregation stand adjacent to the cantor, to this day.

The Yom Kippur Earthly Court

As discussed in the previous chapter, the halakhah requires the *Seliḥot* prayer leader to enwrap himself in the *talit (atifah)*, as he appropriates the role of Hashem, as it were. This same theme repeats itself in the convening of a *beit din*, the Jewish court of law. The Rambam states, "When does judgment start? When the judges wrap themselves and sit in a *talit*" (*Hilkhot Tefillah* 6:6). Judges require *atifah* because of the verse, "The Lord stands in the congregation of God, in the midst of judges He rules..." (Psalms 82:1). The Rambam thus states: "The

Divine Presence accompanies a proper *beit din*. Therefore the judges must sit in fear and awe, being enwrapped [in the *talit*]" (*Hilkhot Sanhedrin* 3:7).

The *beit din* theme recurs in the Yom Kippur *Avodah*. When the *Kohen Gadol* performed the *Avodah*, he was accompanied by two people, the *Sgan* to his right and the *Rosh Beit Av* to his left. Except when lighting the incense within the Holy of Holies, in all other activities the *Kohen Gadol* was accompanied by these two assistants. As a present day reflection of this practice, it is customary for two people to stand by the *ḥazan* during the recitation of Kol Nidrei. The *beit din* motif of Yom Kippur was instituted to emphasize the *lifnei Hashem* relationship. The Creator of the world comes to our minyan and prays with us.

For a *beit din* to have any significance, it must rule on legal issues presented before them. In fact, this *beit din* at Kol Nidrei rules on two points of law:

1) granting permission for the congregation to pray among sinners; and
2) nullification of vows through Kol Nidrei.

However, in a broader sense, this *beit din* is asked to rule on an additional legal issue. The mystery of repentance, whereby previous sins are erased or even elevated to mitzvot,[viii] has engaged Jewish philosophers for centuries. Among the questions they address is whether the granting of forgiveness through repentance is a result of bestowal of Divine grace (*ḥesed*), or rather a result of Divine justice (*mishpat*), a right that man earns through his positive actions.[ix] In this context, the earthly *beit din* must rule: Does man deserve forgiveness or not?

In the first battle between Israel and Amalek, the anticipated outcome was clear: Israel was ultimately to win. However, Hashem did not want the victory to be a pure act of *ḥesed*; the victory needed to be won through *mishpat*. Moses alone was not invested with sufficient authority to make this determination; for this purpose a duly constituted *beit din* was needed that included himself, Aaron, and Ḥur.[x] The Biblical narrative indicates that Aaron and Ḥur supported Moses' arms during the battle "until the sun set" (Exodus 17:12). As a reflection of this incident, the halakhah makes clear that a *beit din* cannot meet at night.

Only after Moses, Aaron, and Ḥur convened did God provide salvation. We can therefore deduce from the Biblical narrative that the Heavenly Court (the *beit din shel ma'alah*) acts only after the earthly *beit din* (*beit din* shel *matah*) provides its own ruling. In accord with this explanation, the Rav emphasized that the version of Kol Nidrei that he recommended reciting mentions the latter before the former *(biyeshivah shel matah uviyeshivah shel ma'alah)*. Within Kol Nidrei, a legal ruling is promulgated which asserts that the assembly is meritorious, that this Yom Kippur will provide complete atonement, and that our prayers will be answered. In this way the atonement provided by Yom Kippur is a duly constituted legal ruling conforming to the requirements of the portion of the *Shulḥan Arukh* dealing with such issues, the *Ḥoshen Mishpat*.

On what halakhic basis does such a *beit din* rule in Israel's merit? Through the wording of the final ruling: "May it be forgiven for the entire congregation (root: *eidah*) of Israel and for the stranger who dwells among them, for the sin befell the entire nation (root: *am*) through error" (Numbers 15:26). Through the Kol Nidrei recitation, Israel is transformed from an entity known as an *eidah* to that of an *am*.

Eidah represents the highest sociological description of a group. An *eidah* is a sophisticated, discerning group of people. An *eidah* understands the difference between good and evil, and comprehends the gravity of sin and its consequences.

On the other hand, *am*, or nation, is an appellation that represents Israel as a collective in its lowest form. As one example of this usage, upon hearing the news of Israel sinning during the Golden Calf incident, Moses was told: "Go descend, for your nation has corrupted itself (*ki shiḥet amkha*)" (Exodus 32:7). The Talmud states: This nation can be compared to dust or [alternatively] to the stars. When they descend [i.e. are unworthy] they descend to the level of dust, and when they ascend, they rise to the level of the stars" (*Megillah* 6b).

The *beit din* realizes that an *eidah* knows full well the consequences of sinning, and recognizes when it has done so. Members of an *eidah* cannot say that they committed the sins in error. How then could atonement apply to such a group? Because the *beit din* in a sense demotes the congregation of Israel from *eidah* to *am*, from an entity that understands sin and its consequences to one which does not. Only for an *am* could sin be considered to have been committed in error.

But what is the basis for the error? A passage in Tractate *Nedarim* (66a) states the following:

> If one vows, "I will not marry this ugly person," and she was [found to be] beautiful, dark complexioned and found to be light, short and found to be tall, she is permitted [for him to marry], not because she was ugly and became beautiful, dark complexioned and came to be light, short and came to be tall, but because the vow was made mistakenly [i.e. under false assumptions].

The Gemara continues:

> There once was an incident where one vowed not to marry his [homely] niece. [The niece] was taken to the house of Rabbi Yishmael, who beautified her. Rabbi Yishmael asked [the one who vowed]: "Is it [indeed] from this [beautiful] woman [you see before you] that you did vow?" He answered, "No," and Rabbi Yishmael released him from his vow. At that moment, Rabbi Yishmael cried and said, "The daughters of Israel are indeed beautiful, but poverty has made them look repulsive."

Israel performs many transgressions which lower her prestige, but the motivation to sin always stems from some external influence. "The daughters of Israel are indeed beautiful": the sin does not enter the personality per se; the sin is a stain that can be washed off.

This analogy recurs in the *kinot* (elegies) of Tishah b'Av. A story is told of how Elijah happened upon a poor, dirty woman. When he asked her identity, she replied that she was the "Congregation of Israel." Elijah responded that if she were to simply wash herself she could once again regain her beauty.

This is the basis of the ruling of the *beit din* during Kol Nidrei. All Jews have acted in error, but they remain fundamentally meritorious. Hashem may, God forbid, initially vow that due to the sinner's repulsiveness He will have nothing to do with him. The *beit din* through their Kol Nidrei ruling abets Hashem, as it were, to absolve His vow.

Hatarat Nedarim is the ritual whereby one retroactively transforms a willful vow into a mistaken one. If we have the power as individuals to alter vows in this way, then we can likewise transform all our sins from willful to mistaken by affirming: "The daughters of Israel are indeed beautiful." This is the declaration that Hashem desires from us on Yom Kippur night. Only then does a Jew have permission to bless God by reciting the *Sheheheyanu* blessing at Kol Nidrei's conclusion for allowing us to live to see this day.[xi]

NOTES

[i] This topic is a major theme in the essay על אהבת התורה וגאולת נפש הדור

[ii] It is interesting to note that the Rav in a previous *teshuvah derashah* similarly lamented the lack of appreciation for the significance of Erev Shabbat:

> Even in those neighborhoods made up predominantly of religious Jews, one can no longer talk of the "sanctity of Shabbat." True, there are Jews in America who observe Shabbat... But it is not for Shabbat that my heart aches; it is for the forgotten "erev Shabbat" (eve of the Sabbath). There are Shabbat-observing Jews in America, but there are no "erev Shabbat" Jews who go out to greet Shabbat with beating hearts and pulsating souls. There are many who observe the precepts with their hands, with their feet, and/or with their mouths -- but there are few indeed who truly know the meaning of the service of the heart!" (*On Repentance*, "The Power of Confession").

[iii] Although the Rav did not say so explicitly in the *derashah*, this concept would obviate the first difficulty in the Rambam as well. Since Erev Yom Kippur is appended to Yom Kippur, the *vidui* of *Minḥah* could indeed be Biblical in origin, as the Rambam implies.

[iv] Apparently, this is the Rav's own explanation of the verse in Leviticus as the basis for the Ramban's view.

[v] The opinion of the Ramban sheds light on a somewhat puzzling passage in *On Repentance*, "Acquittal and Purification."

> ...the confession of the Minḥah (afternoon) service on the eve of Yom Kippur, <u>whose purpose is purification</u> (annotator's emphasis) is not recited by the synagogue reader, "for one cannot appoint an intermediary for purification." Every Jew must enter within   the

"holiness of the day" as an individual and stand as he is "before God." As the nightfall of Yom Kippur approaches, each person listens to the inner voice that calls on us to "be cleansed."

[vi] See *On Repentance*, "The Individual and the Community."

[vii] The Rav expounds on this theme in footnote 108 of *Halakhic Man* (p. 156), where he cites a passage from *Bereishit Rabbah* combined with various Talmudic sources as the basis for the analogy between *tohu vavohu,* evil and Amalek.

[viii] See *On Repentance*, "Blotting Out Evil or Elevating It."

[ix] See *On Repentance*, "Acquittal and Purification," where the Rav discusses this issue at length.

[x] See Rashi on Exodus 17:10 and *Orah Hayyim* 619:4.

[xi] It is most interesting to note that at this point in the lecture, the Rav emphasized that his discussion of the *beit din* motif on Yom Kippur is the most textually consistent [*oisgehalten*] of any other topic he had discussed in any of his previous *teshuvah derashot.* He emphasized that this motif "is not homiletical, is not *drush* but rather *amito shel halakhah.*"

Rabbi Akiva's Homily on *Teshuvah**

The final mishnah in Tractate *Yoma* concludes with the following:

> Rabbi Akiva said: Happy are you, O Israel! Before whom are you purified and who purifies you? Your Father in Heaven, as it is stated: "And I will sprinkle on you purifying waters and you shall be cleansed, and it states, "Hashem is the hope [lit. 'Mikveh'] of Israel": just as a mikveh purifies the impure, so does the Holy One Blessed Be He purify Israel.

In reading this passage, one is struck by the apparent superfluity of Rabbi Akiva's statement and a number of questions therefore come to mind: What was Rabbi Akiva's *ḥiddush*, what

* BASED ON THE 1973 AND 1975 *TESHUVAH DERASHOT*

new lesson was he illuminating in his homily? Who else besides
God could grant purification on Yom Kippur? Why did Rabbi
Akiva find it necessary to cite two separate verses to buttress what
prima facie would seem to be such an obvious point? Furthermore,
why is Hashem referred to as "Your Father in Heaven" specifically
in this context? Why the repetition in the phrase, "before whom are
you purified and who purifies you?" Why does Rabbi Akiva
deviate from the simple translation of the word "mikveh" as
meaning "hope" to a more strained literal translation implying
ritual immersion?

In his annual *teshuvah derashot*, the Rav rarely missed an
opportunity to expound on the aforementioned mishnah as a means
of amplifying specific themes in these lectures.

MEDIATED AND UNMEDIATED ATONEMENT

There is an apparent inconsistency in the Rambam's *Hilkhot
Teshuvah* regarding the prescription for attaining atonement during
and after the Temple period. The Rambam submits the following as
the means for atonement during the Temple period:

> ...those who have committed sins and trespasses, at the time that
> they bring their sacrifices for their accidental or willful sin, they
> are not atoned with their sacrifice until they repent and confess
> orally, as the verse states: "And they shall confess that which they
> sinned over it." And so all those who are obliged to die through
> court decree and those obliged to obtain lashes are not atoned
> through their death or lashes until they repent and confess. And
> similarly, one who injures his friend or damages his property,
> even though he has made restitution, he is not atoned until he
> confesses and repents from ever doing a similar act forever....The
> scapegoat (*sa'ir hamishtalei'aḥ*), because it is an atonement for
> all Israel, the *Kohen Gadol* offers a confession over it in the name
> of all Israel. The scapegoat atones for all transgressions...
> (*Hilkhot Teshuvah* 1:1-2).

The essential message is that although there were numerous ritual means to attain atonement during the time of the Temple, none of them were operative without *teshuvah* as a prerequisite.

This concept contrasts with the very next halakhah of the *Mishneh Torah*:

> Nowadays that the Temple no longer exists and there is no altar to atone, there is only repentance; and repentance atones for everything. Even if one was evil all his days and repented at the very end, none of the evil is remembered...and the day of Yom Kippur itself (*itzumo shel yom*) atones for repenters (*lashavim*), as the verse states: "For through this day atonement shall be made for you..." (*Hilkhot Teshuvah* 1:3).

Now, after the Temple period, *teshuvah* no longer serves merely as a prerequisite to atonement. Instead, *teshuvah* itself becomes the means through which atonement is attained. Moreover, a new means of atonement is introduced here by the Rambam: the *itzumo shel yom.*

The Rambam's message regarding Yom Kippur in the two halakhot cited is based on specific Biblical passages. The fact that communal atonement was attained on Yom Kippur during the time of the Temple through the *sa'ir hamishtalei'ah* is based on the Biblical verse: "And the goat shall bear upon him all their sins [and remove them] to an uninhabited land" (Leviticus 16:22). Today, however, during a time when the *sa'ir hamishtalei'ah* no longer exists, the means to contemporary atonement is described by the verse: "Because through[i] this day (*bayom*) He will forgive you, to purify you from all your sins, before Hashem you shall be purified...." (Leviticus 16:30). The word *bayom* in this case does not mean "*on* this day" as it is usually translated. Instead, it means "*through* this day." The day itself provides the atonement.

Although a precise understanding of the nature of *itzumo shel yom* is elusive, it is understood that the capability of the day of

Yom Kippur to effect atonement for an individual is in direct proportion to the holiness that the Jew himself experiences on Yom Kippur. The power of Yom Kippur to provide atonement as directly proportional to the holiness one imputes to it is described in the *Tefillah Zakkah* meditation where Yom Kippur is described as: "A powerful day of the year, a great day of the year, a day that is sanctified above all others." The power of Yom Kippur to forgive is juxtaposed with the holiness that is imparted through sanctification of the day itself by individual Jews. Should Yom Kippur be treated like any other day, then the atonement afforded by the *itzumo shel yom* is insubstantial.

The power of the *itzumo shel yom* is therefore the essential message of Rabbi Akiva. A demoralized nation that could not imagine a Yom Kippur without the various Temple rituals was told that a new type of atonement could be readily attained. The Yom Kippur Temple service was an intricate ritual accomplished by the High Priest, in the same way that involved protocols are generally required before a commoner approaches a king. However, the atonement of the *itzumo shel yom* no longer requires intricate ceremonies; our approach to God can now be unmediated and as direct as a son's approach to his own father.

Although the term "before Hashem" is indeed used at certain points in the Biblical description of the *Avodah* ritual (e.g. Leviticus 16:13, "he shall place the incense upon the fire before Hashem"), also suggesting an unmediated approach, one should note that in describing the *Avodah*, the phrase is used specifically in the context of God as King as opposed to Father. In contrast, Rabbi Akiva is stating that the approach today is unencumbered by elaborate rituals, since the relationship is now one of a father to a son: "your Father in heaven."

The role of *teshuvah* has thus been transformed since the Temple's destruction. The function of *teshuvah* has changed from being the prerequisite for atonement to being the very source of atonement.[1] Today, *teshuvah* affords the same atonement accomplished by sacrifices in the Temple period: "Repentance atones for everything...."

THE *DEREKH TESHUVAH*

In ancient times, the very atmosphere surrounding Jerusalem and the Temple served to inspire Jews to do *teshuvah*. The prophet Jonah received his prophetic calling during a moment of particular inspiration at a *Simḥat Beit Hasho'evah,* the joyful ritual of drawing water to pour on the altar during the holiday of Sukkot (*Yerushalmi Sukkah* 55a). The inspiration one gained from merely observing this event motivated repentance. The means through which one effectively engaged in the act of *teshuvah* was eminently clear, the road towards repentance sure and unequivocal.

Today, in contrast, as the Temple lies desolate, the path towards repentance or the *derekh teshuvah* has become obscure. How does one effectively engage in this activity?

This problem of the *derekh teshuvah* is discussed by the Rambam in *Hilkhot Teshuvah,* in his description of the Ten Days of Repentance:

> And for this reason the entire House of Israel has the custom to maximize charity and good deeds, and to engage in mitzvah

---

[1] The Rambam in the latter halakhah states: "Nowadays there is only *teshuvah.*" Why not, "Nowadays there is only *vidui*" to parallel the first halakhah, where *vidui* accompanied the scapegoat ritual? During the time of the Temple, the atonement ritual included *vidui,* while today the atonement itself occurs through *teshuvah.* The atonement was a sacrifice over which, as part of the ritual, *vidui* was recited. In contrast, one cannot refer to a "sacrifice over which *teshuvah* was done"; *teshuvah* was not part of the atonement ritual. Similarly, today *vidui* is not a part of the atonement per se; it is an intrinsic part of *teshuvah* itself (see *On Repentance,* "The Power of Confession").

performance from Rosh Hashanah until Yom Kippur more than the rest of the year (3:4).

Yom Kippur is a time for repentance for all, for an individual and for many, and it is the culmination of pardon and forgiveness for Israel. Therefore, all are obligated to repent and confess on Yom Kippur (2:7).

The Rambam thus suggests that the *derekh teshuvah* during the Ten Days of Repentance apparently consists first of doing mitzvot, which only later is followed by actual repentance as Yom Kippur approaches.

However, Rabbi Israel Salanter suggested that the Rambam's *derekh teshuvah* sequence should actually be reversed; the performance of mitzvot should come after repentance rather than before. The prescription of mitzvah performance as the precursor to *teshuvah* itself would seem to be inconsistent with scriptural intent as well. On the verse: "For Hashem your God, he is God of gods and Lord of lords, the great God, mighty and awesome, Who does not regard people nor take bribes..." (Deuteronomy 10:17), the Ramban (Naḥmanides) implies a basic question: how can the concept of bribery even remotely be applied to the Master of the Universe? The Ramban answers that the "bribe" is in fact the performance of mitzvot. Hashem does not accept mitzvot in lieu of punishment, even from an otherwise righteous individual.

Elsewhere, in fact, the Rambam himself seems to disparage mitzvot as a means towards atonement. According to the Rambam, one who has sinned repeatedly, "...cries out [in supplication] and is not answered, as the verse states: 'Even if they engage in copious prayer I will not listen,' and if one does mitzvot [under such conditions] they are ripped up before him" (*Hilkhot Teshuvah* 7:7). In other words, the mitzvot "bounce" and do no good for the sinner. If so, what then is the explanation for the suggested sequence of the earlier passage from the *Mishneh Torah*?

Despite the apparent inconsistencies, the *derekh teshuvah* of the Rambam (mitzvah performance followed by repentance) does in fact find an echo in the *Yalkut Shimoni*: "'Return O Israel unto Hashem your God' -- All who have in their hands an act of transgression and are ashamed to do *teshuvah* should substitute it for a good deed and [then] do *teshuvah*" (*Yalkut Shimoni [Nevi'im]* 529). Sometimes external circumstances render *teshuvah* very difficult to do. Entire families can be transgressors, and separation from their sinful ways is very hard. The *Yalkut Shimoni* gives the advice that good deeds can precede *teshuvah* when immediate *teshuvah* is too arduous: "This is analogous to one who has bad coins (*zuzim*); he can go to a storekeeper and present them along with some extra money and exchange them for good ones. Similarly, all who have bad actions should repent and do good actions."

What are "bad *zuzim*" and "bad actions"? The *Yalkut Shimoni* here clearly does not refer to sins, because "bad *zuzim*" have some intrinsic value as currency while sins have no value at all. We must therefore deduce that the *Yalkut Shimoni* must be referring to the mitzvot of a sinner.[2] The lesson is that a person should first accumulate mitzvot or "bad *zuzim*" so that through *teshuvah* they will ultimately be exchanged for a better currency.

The reason for the suggested sequence of good deeds followed by *teshuvah* as presented by the Rambam lies in the fundamental psychology of the sinner. Sin emanates from two sources, suggested homiletically in the Biblical description of Cain after the murder of his brother: "And Cain was very angry and his countenance fell" (Genesis 4:5). Sometimes sin results from anger. Why was Cain angry? Because Abel's sacrificial gift was accepted, while his was rejected. When confronted with God's rejection, Cain could not accept the implicit rebuke. Cain's maintained that

---

[2]R. Yosef Ber Soloveitchik (the *Beit HaLevi*) alluded to a similar thought in the introduction to his *Ḥumash* commentary.

his own understanding was always unerring, even in religious matters.

Accepting the yoke of mitzvot requires subservience and submittal to the Divine Will. In Rashi's words: "One has no permission to question [their significance]" (Rashi on Numbers 19:2). Hashem's statutes cannot be rationalized, and their value cannot be judged.[ii] Cain sinned because he thought that his cognition could supplant Hashem's.

The category of people who cannot subjugate themselves before the Higher Will is referred to in the *Aleinu* prayer (recited in the *Malkhuyot* section of the Rosh Hashanah *Amidah*) as *rish'ei aretz*, the wicked of the land.[3] To change their status, they must learn, "...for to You will every knee bend, will every tongue swear," to bend one's will to Hashem. These *rish'ei aretz* are represented by the ox sacrificed by the *Kohen Gadol* during the Yom Kippur *Avodah*. An ox represents one who is deluded by his own perceived greatness, as the verse states: "Much increase is by the strength of the ox" (Proverbs 14:4).

Yet, aside from the *rish'ei aretz*, there is another, opposite type of sinner, alluded to in the latter phrase of the verse in Genesis: "and his countenance fell." Here sin results not out of arrogance, but rather out of self-negation. This type of sinner is subservient to everything and everyone. He is a spiritual wanderer -- he does not want to sin, yet submits to temptation; he wants to repent but feels that he cannot; he senses the call of holiness, but does not answer. This type of sinner is referred to as *b'nei basar,* literally "children of the flesh."

To represent this type of sinner, the *Kohen Gadol* offered a ram, reminiscent of the ram caught in the bush in the *Akedah*

---

[3]The Rav referred specifically to communist leaders as fitting this description. While reading communist literature, one is struck immediately by the "chutzpah" of its leadership. Communism is a system wherein its followers, and certainly its leaders, can never admit to mistakes.

incident. The *b'nei basar* type of sinner becomes entangled in the obstacles of life, in the thorns and dry grass, from which he cannot extricate himself.[4]

There is a passage in the Talmud *(Avodah Zarah* 17a) that illustrates this weakling type of sinner: "It was said of Elazar the son of Durdya that there was no prostitute in the world whom he had not frequented...." The Gemara here depicts an addict to sin, and continues: "He went and sat between two mountains and hills. He said, "Mountains and hills, request mercy for me.' They replied: 'Before we request [mercy] on your behalf, we must request it on our own behalf,' as the verse states 'the mountains may depart and the hills may be removed....'" (Isaiah 54:10).

The tragedy of the weakling type of sinner is that he indeed wishes to attain forgiveness, but asks others to do the job for him. Their response must be that only the sinner himself can accomplish this goal.

One of the greatest mercies that God bestows on man on Yom Kippur is His perception of us not as arrogant sinners, but rather as weakling sinners, for were it otherwise, favorable judgment would be impossible.

We can now understand why the Rambam, echoing the *Yalkut Shimoni*, suggests that the *derekh teshuvah* consists of mitzvah fulfillment followed by *teshuvah* itself. The second mishnah of *Rosh Hashanah* describes God's judgment on this day in the following way: "All inhabitants of the world pass before him as members of the flock" *(kivnei maron)*. Resh Lakish in the Gemara clarifies the words *kivnei maron* to mean a narrow entry through which only one can enter at a time *(Rosh Hashanah* 18a). The sinner enters into this small pass, and as he observes more mitzvot he gains self-confidence and his yearning for holiness grows. His character and

---

[4]The two descriptions of *rish'ei aretz* and *b'nei basar* are also halakhic categories: "apostate due to spite," (מומר להכעיס); and "apostate due to temptation," (מומר לתיאבון) *(Avodah Zarah* 26b).

will become strengthened so when Yom Kippur arrives, *teshuvah* comes almost naturally. This passage thus reflects the Rambam's sequence of good deeds followed by *teshuvah* as the *derekh teshuvah*.

"Sprinkling" on Rosh Hashanah/ "Immersion" on Yom Kippur

The importance of mitzvah performance specifically in reference to Rosh Hashanah is described by the Rambam:

> Just as the merits of a person are weighed against his sins at the time of his death, so every year each individual's sins are weighed against his merits on the holiday of Rosh Hashanah (*Hilkhot Teshuvah* 3:3).

> Even though the blowing of the shofar on Rosh Hashanah is a decree of the Torah, there is an [additional] inference in it [with the message]: "Awake sleepers from your sleep and slumberers from your slumber...." Therefore, every individual is obligated to see himself the entire year as half-meritorious and half-guilty, and because of this, the entire House of Israel maintains the custom of increasing charity, good deeds, and involvement in mitzvot from Rosh Hashanah until Yom Kippur more than the rest of the year (*Hilkhot Teshuvah* 3:4).

The Rav highlighted a difficulty in the textual flow of these halakhot. After introducing the concept of balancing mitzvot and transgressions particularly in regard to Rosh Hashanah, the Rambam interrupts the thought and discusses how the concept applies to the entire year. Only then does the Rambam again return to discussion of Rosh Hashanah and Yom Kippur.

The reason for this unusual sequence lies first in understanding the role of the shofar. One may mistakenly infer from the Rambam that the shofar acts as a source of reproof. Yet God, in speaking to the prophet Isaiah, states: "Lift your voice as a shofar, and declare unto My nation their transgression" (Isaiah 58:1). If the shofar is itself a source of reproof, why should the prophet not simply blow a shofar to accomplish this goal?

In the book of Jonah the narrative tells how the prophet fell asleep while the ship on which he was a passenger was in danger of being destroyed by a severe storm. The captain of the ship awakened Jonah with the words: "How can you sleep so soundly? Arise, and call on your God!" (Jonah 1:6). The shofar's role is analogous to that of the ship's captain as he addressed Jonah. There is no specific lesson that the shofar suggests; just wake up! The shofar prompts what the Rav calls crisis-awareness. We are in crisis because the fate of the individual as well as that of the world is in a precarious state of balance. The appropriate action can change the outcome to our favor.

The consciousness regarding one being "half meritorious and half guilty" is a permanent feature throughout the year, but on Rosh Hashanah, the day of judgment, there is a greater sense of urgency to act. *Teshuvah* is therefore not our primary concern on Rosh Hashanah. There is a more pressing need to maximize mitzvot and hence tip the scales of survival to our favor.[5]

The importance of maintaining a plurality of mitzvot over transgressions is based on a well-defined halakhic principle called *rubo kekulo* -- "a majority is equivalent to its entirety." As an example of this principle, the Rosh maintains that if one bites into two kosher items and one non-kosher item simultaneously, he has not committed a transgression.[6] In other words, a prohibited entity

---

[5] Because of the need to maximize mitzvot after Rosh Hashanah, the Vilna Gaon ruled that *kiddush levanah* for the month of Tishri, which is normally said after Yom Kippur, should in fact be recited during the Ten Days of Repentance.

[6] ‏רא"ש חולין פ"ז סימן לז‎. The ‏רמ"א‎ quotes this opinion as halakhah. (‏סי' קט‎ ‏(טור יו"ד‎

becomes part of a larger entity that is permitted. A second example of the application of this concept is in the field of court rulings. If in a *beit din* of three judges, two maintain a defendant's innocence while one maintains his guilt, the court acquits. The acquittal results from the ruling provided by a judicial body as a single entity that transcends the individual opinion of its members.[7]

The halakhic principles that govern a Jew's activities on earth similarly govern God's relationship to the Jew. As a result, on a metaphysical level the same concept of *rubo kekulo* applies on Rosh Hashanah. If an individual's transgressions are in the minority, then they become absorbed into the mitzvah majority, rendering the person righteous. The Rambam emphasizes that this concept is operative from Rosh Hashanah through the remainder of the days before Yom Kippur.

Yom Kippur, however, works according to an entirely different standard. Hashem no longer uses the principle of *rubo kekulo;* He demands total purification.[8] Man must be clear of sin to come out whole in the judgment process of Yom Kippur.   Therefore, *teshuvah* is now necessary, for it is impossible to be without blemish unless the existing blemishes are removed.

For this reason, the Rambam states that "the day of Yom Kippur itself atones for returnees (*lashavim*)." He does not say that the day of Yom Kippur atones "with *teshuvah*." The entire person must be a "returnee." The necessity for complete *teshuvah* is the reason that Rabbi Akiva used the mikveh analogy in his homily. A mikveh serves to purify the entire person. If one finger lacks

---

[7] סנהדרין ג: תוס׳ ב״ק כז: ד״ה קמ״ל ,וחידושי הגר״ח על הש״ס ("סטנסיל") שם

[8] As a halakhic analogy for this principle, the Rambam holds that the four cups of wine on Passover must be drunk in their entirety: one has not fulfilled the mitzvah unless the cups are totally consumed. (This is the *lekhathilah* position of the Rambam, reflected as well in the *Shulḥan Arukh*, although *post facto [bedi'eved]* one still fulfills his obligation through drinking the majority of the cups.)

contact with the mikveh water, the purification does not take place and, as a result, no part of the person is pure (*Yoreh De'ah* 198:1).

The words of Rabbi Akiva are therefore quite precise in this description: "... just as a mikveh purifies the impure, [exactly] so does the Holy One Blessed Be He purify Israel," analogous to the relationship of the sprinkling of water (*haza'ah*) to immersion in the water (*tevilah*). Rabbi Akiva thus refers to both steps in the mishnah in sequence: "'and I will sprinkle on you purifying waters and you shall be cleansed,' and it states: 'Hashem is the hope (lit. 'mikveh') of Israel.'" [iii]

One who is impure by reason of contact with a dead body requires both *haza'ah* and *tevilah* (Numbers 19:1-12). The purpose of the sprinkling is to prepare one for the later immersion. Mitzvah performance is therefore part of the *derekh teshuvah* which takes place during the nine days from Rosh Hashanah until the day before Yom Kippur, and is a prerequisite to *teshuvah*.

YOM KIPPUR: GOD IN SEARCH OF MAN

Yom Kippur has a significance distinct from the nine days prior to it. On Yom Kippur, God comes closest to man. The closer His approach, the greater the *teshuvah* obligation, as the prophet states: "Call Him while He is close" (Isaiah 55:6). On Yom Kippur, Hashem calls man by name, mirroring the very first Yom Kippur when Hashem Himself waited for Moses on Mount Sinai: "And Hashem descended in a cloud and stood with him there..." (Exodus 34:5).

On Yom Kippur, Hashem knocks on the door of every Jew.[9][iv] It therefore becomes incumbent on us to practice the mitzvah of *hakhnasat orḥim* -- the welcoming of guests – the guest being

---

[9] This is a major theme in the Song of Songs (5:2): פתחי לי רעיתי יונתי תמתי "Open to me my sister, my love, my dove...".

Hashem Himself. Hashem yearns to be close to His people on Yom Kippur.[10]

In light of this understanding we may discern a new reason for the choice of the *Haftarah* portion read on Yom Kippur. The *Haftarah* of the four fasts contains the exhortation of Isaiah: "Search for Hashem when He is to be found, call on Him when He is close...."(Isaiah 55:6). In contrast, the *Haftarah* for Yom Kippur is taken from another chapter in Isaiah that includes the passage: "Cast up, cast up, prepare the way [*solu solu panu derekh*], lift the stumbling block from the path of My people" (Isaiah 57:14). Although both chapters are clearly relevant to Yom Kippur, it would initially appear that the first selection would be more appropriate. After all, the Rambam explicitly identifies the initial verse as referring to the Ten Days of Repentance (*Hilkhot Teshuvah* 2:5).

Although Rashi (*Megillah* 31a) presents a reason that *solu* is designated as the *Haftarah*,[11] the Rav suggested another explanation.

---

[10] In the opinion of Rebbe, this yearning is so strong that *teshuvah* is not even required in order to attain atonement on Yom Kippur (*Shevuot* 13a).

[11] The reason given by Rashi (s.v. *ki koh*) is that the doctrine of *tzom*, or fasting, appears in this passage. The prophet exhorts the people that the fast of Yom Kippur must be accompanied by true repentance as opposed to the simple act of abstaining from food. Another reason given is that the specific mitzvah of honor (*kibud*) for Yom Kippur appears in this selection: "and if you call the Sabbath a delight, the holy of the Lord as honored ..." (Isaiah 58:13). Although this verse forms the basis for the mitzvah of *oneg Shabbat*, involving eating and drinking on the Sabbath, according to the Gemara the last three words, "the holy of the Lord as honored" (*mekhubad*), refers to the special mitzvah of honoring Yom Kippur, accomplished through the donning of fresh clothing, for example. [See chapter on "Approach and Arrival of Yom Kippur"]

When the Jew must "search for God when He can be found," the initiative for the search rests entirely with man. The next verse in Isaiah contains the phrase, "let him return to God"; return is up to man. This path to God is not a highway but rather a narrow, winding, and challenging road, reflecting the nature of *teshuvah* throughout the year.

On Yom Kippur, in contrast, God comes forward to meet man. Hashem facilitates the way for Israel's return: He takes us by the hand and shows us how to do *teshuvah.* He removes all obstacles and transforms an otherwise tortuous road into a straight highway: *panu derekh.* In a spiritually desolate world we can easily become disoriented, losing our sense of reality. We are remote from repentance both intellectually and emotionally. In this wilderness, Hashem appears to show us the road home. Suddenly, the normally arduous *teshuvah* process presents no hardship at all. We hear His whisper: *solu solu panu derekh.*

To further prove this point, the Rav again turned to Rabbi Akiva's homily: "Rabbi Akiva said: 'Happy are you Israel: before whom are you purified and who purifies you: your Father in Heaven.'" Generally speaking, God grants atonement as an act of grace, while man through his own effort attains purification through *teshuvah.*[v] In *On Repentance,* "Expiation, Suffering and Redemption," the Rav describes the difference between atonement and purification as follows:

> Kaparah (acquittal) affects the removal of punishment. The "indemnity payment" shields man from Divine anger and wrath. However, his personality remains contaminated, and this condition can only be remedied through ritual "immersion," that is, by wholehearted repentance. Purification is conditional upon our drawing near and standing directly "before God," and, as such, it is a spiritually uplifting experience...[I]n the time of the Temple...the High Priest would "direct his attention to those who were assembled," and say, in effect: "We, the Temple priests, are engaged in the performance of those precepts which concern the

> sacrificial service of the day of Yom Kippur whereby acquittal of sin, *kaparah,* is granted. However, the act of purification is something you must perform by yourselves, each man in his own heart." And he would then say: "Be you cleansed!"

However, the message of Rabbi Akiva is that God so desires His people's closeness on Yom Kippur that ultimately God Himself effects purification as well. Thus the double phrasing of Rabbi Akiva: "before whom are you purified" [i.e. through man's actions] "and who purifies you" [i.e. through God's action].

Why does God go to such lengths to facilitate our return? Simply because the Creator has mercy on His creation. As the prophet further states:

> For I will not contend eternally, and I will not be angry forever, because the spirit that enwraps itself is from Me, and souls which I have made. For the sin of his covetousness was I angry, and smote him: I hid Myself and was angry, and he [continued] to go aimlessly in the ways of his heart. I have seen his ways and I will heal him, I will lead him and restore comfort to him and to his mourners (Isaiah 57:16-18).

Reflecting this theme, we recite the following phrase during *Seliḥot*: "The soul is Yours, and the body is Your work: have mercy on Your handiwork." The Rambam has said that this is one of the greatest of the prayers for mercy, for how can He possibly continue to be angry at His own creation?

As the Red Sea was split, the angels questioned God: since both the Israelites as well as the Egyptians were idolaters, why did the Israelites merit redemption? The answer is that the Israelites were already steeped in the deepest level of impurity and had He tarried an extra moment, there would no longer have been a Jewish people. Sometimes Hashem forgives our sins not because we merit forgiveness, but because without such forgiveness we would be forever lost.

The establishment of the State of Israel is a contemporary example of God's intervention to an undeserving generation. Although previous generations of Jewish leadership were spiritually exalted, why did Hashem see fit to bestow the State of Israel to our generation, in an age of religious and moral midgets, as it were? The reason is that earlier generations did not need a State of Israel for their Judaism to survive. Ezekiel was able to experience God in exile, in a concentration camp in Babylonia. In contrast, without a State of Israel today the Jewish people would be lost in a tidal wave of assimilation.

Hashem approaches man on Yom Kippur because, in a real sense, He has no choice. He is compelled to forgive His people: "Peace, peace to him that is distant and that is near, says Hashem…and I will heal him" (Isaiah 57:19).

NOTES

[i] In his *teshuvah derashot*, the Rav consistently translated the phrase
כי ביום הזה..., "for <u>through</u> this day" rather than "for <u>on</u> this day." The
preposition ב in this context is known grammatically as the בי"ת הכלי, the
"instrumental ב." As an example of such use of the letter ב, the Rav cited
the מורה נבוכים of the Rambam, who translates the preposition in the word
בראשית in a similar way:

והעולם לא נברא בראשית זמנית...כי הזמן בכלל הנבראים. ולפיכך אמר בראשית ,
                                                 והבי"ת ענין 'פי' .

A detailed description of use of the "ב *instrumenti*" can be found in
Gesinius' Hebrew Grammar (Oxford 1909) p. 380, (119 l-q) note 6. See
also endnote ii in the chapter "The Day of Yom Kippur as the Medium of
Atonement".

[ii] This same theme was the topic of a lecture the Rav presented to the
Rabbinical Council of America in 1972 on the *Aseret Hadibrot* (The Ten
Commandments). The lecture is essentially transcribed in *Nora'ot Harav*,
Volume 5, pp. 31-52, and summarized in *Shiurei Harav*.

[iii] The second verse is not introduced by the word ונאמר but rather ואומר.
The Rav emphasized this difference in his lecture but without explanation.
The Rav apparently suggested that use of the word ואומר in this context
emphasizes a chronology or process: the second verse suggests a second
stage in the process which must be preceded by the first stage implied in
the first verse.

[iv] In another context, the imagery of the Song of Songs in its description of
God knocking on the door of His beloved, forms the basis for two of the
Rav's most acclaimed essays: *Kol Dodi Dofek*, and *Uvikashtem Misham*.

[v] For an explanation of the *Kapparah-Taharah* dichotomy in this context,
see *On Repentance*, "Acquital and Purification."

The Significance of the Various Appellations for Yom Kippur[*]

The poetry of Rabbi Elazar Hakallir forms the bulk of the *piyyutim* (liturgical poems) that we recite on the *Yamim Nora'im* (Days of Awe). He had the ability to weave Biblical allusions into soaring verse that is at the same time metrically firm and thematically consonant. His *piyyutim* have, for many centuries, set the tone for the powerful *Yamim Nora'im* experience. According to the Rav, the words of Rabbi Elazar Hakallir are not merely lyrical accoutrements to the Days of Awe, but contain halakhic significance as well.

Through an analysis of the various names that the liturgist uses to refer to Yom Kippur, one can begin to appreciate the singular nature of the day. In the initial portion of the repetition of the *Musaf*

---

* BASED ON THE 1976 AND 1977 *TESHUVAH DERASHOT*

Amidah Rabbi Elazar Hakallir makes use of three appellations in referring to the day of Yom Kippur :

נחשב כצג באיתון, דחות בפלולי עקלתון, ונקדישך *בשבת שבתון*, קדוש
היום בפתחך ספרים, חן אום שמך מפארים, ונקדישך *ביום הכפורים*, קדוש
מסטין בכבל אסור, ותקות אסירי בשור, ונקדישך *בצום העשור*, קדוש

May we be considered as one who stood at the entry gate [of the Temple courtyard]
So that our prayer can repulse the corrupt serpent [i.e. the evil inclination]
And let us sanctify You on this *Shabbat Shabbaton* (Sabbath of Sabbaths), O Holy One

Today when You open Your books [of life and death]
Be gracious to the nation that glorifies Your Name
And let us sanctify You on this *Yom HaKippurim* (Day of Atonement), O Holy One

Restrain the adversary in chains
And herald the hope of captives
And let us sanctify You on this *Tzom He'asor* (Fast of the Tenth), O Holy One

In this *piyyut,* the day of Yom Kippur is referred to alternately as *Shabbat Shabbaton, Yom HaKippurim,* and *Tzom He'asor.* The Rav's 1977 *teshuvah derashah* centered on the significance of each of these three appellations.[i] His *derashah* focused initially on the second appellation, *Yom HaKippurim.*

YOM HAKIPPURIM

Yom HaKippurim versus Yom Kapparah

The plural form, *kippurim,* has an entirely different meaning from the singular form, *kapparah.* The term *Yom Kapparah* as an appellation for Yom Kippur would contain two misleading implications.

First, *kapparah* implies animal sacrifice as in, for example, *heivi kapparato* (*Horayot* 4a). If the holiday were to be known as *Yom Kapparah*, one might mistakenly reach the conclusion that it is a day dedicated entirely to animal sacrifice. Yet, in reality there were far fewer sacrifices offered in the Temple on Yom Kippur than there were, for instance, on each of the first two days of Sukkot. The term *Yom Kapparah* would therefore be imprecise.[1]

In addition, if we were to emphasize the element of animal sacrifice through use of the appellation, *Yom Kapparah*, the day would carry diminished significance since the destruction of the Temple. Yet, the Rambam clearly states: "Now that there is no Temple and no altar atonement there is only repentance; repentance atones for all sins..." (*Hilkhot Teshuvah* 1:3).

The day of Yom Kippur itself embodies the opportunity for complete atonement exactly as it did prior to the destruction of the Temple.[2] When the repentance is proper, one attains the very same level of *kapparah* as the Jew who stood in the *azarah* and responded, *Barukh shem kevod malkhuto le'olam va'ed* upon hearing the ineffable Name recited by the *Kohen Gadol*.

Another implication of the name *Yom Kapparah* would be a day in which atonement is bestowed upon us by God. Such an emphasis would be inconsistent with the names of the other holidays, since these other names invariably serve to highlight the obligations incumbent on the Jew. For example, Passover is

---

[1] It could be argued, however, that the number of sacrifices on Yom Kippur specifically designated as sin offerings exceeds the number offered on other days of the year.

[2] In contrast to Yom Kippur, the *shalosh regalim* (the three festivals) do not have the same holiness today as they did during the Temple's existence, since today there are no *korbanot* and there is no Temple pilgrimage.

referred to not as *Ḥag Yetzi'at Mitzrayim* , but rather, as *Ḥag HaMatzot*, the emphasis being on the mitzvah most closely associated with the holiday. Similarly, the holiday of Shavuot is bound to the mitzvah of *sefirat ha'omer*.[3] Sukkot is the holiday in which we are obligated to dwell in booths. *Yom HaZikaron* (Rosh Hashanah) refers to *zikhron teruah*, a day on which we must blow the shofar.

Therefore, to be consistent with the other holidays, the designation for Yom Kippur must reflect the fact that through this day atonement is to be attained by man, and not automatically granted by God. As an example of this active usage of the term, the Gemara states: "The table of a person atones" (*Berakhot* 55a), in that the conduct of eating the meal is a means of attaining *kapparah*. The term *kippur* therefore suggests a specific action the Jew must perform to attain atonement.

This dichotomy between *kapparah* and *kippurim* is suggested in the Yom Kippur *Amidah*: "And You gave us, Hashem our God, with love this *Yom Hakippurim* for pardon, forgiveness, and atonement ('*ulekhaparah*')." Thus *kippurim* must differ from the word *ulekhaparah*; otherwise the latter would be superfluous in this context (i.e., "And You gave us...this Day of Atonement for pardon, forgiveness, and atonement") . *Yom HaKippurim* signifies a day on which the Jew must perform specific actions to attain atonement, while the three terms, *seliḥah, meḥilah,* and *kapparah,* refer to Hashem's response to those actions.

---

[3] In the *Vatitein lanu* paragraph of the *Amidah,* only after using the appellations *Ḥag HaMatzot* and *Ḥag HaShavuot*, are the days described as *Zeman Heiruteinu* or *Zeman Matan Torateinu*. The human imperative always precedes the historical description of these holidays.

In light of the *Mishneh Torah* passage quoted above, the act by which man attains atonement is, of course, repentance.[4] The term *kippurim* therefore refers specifically to repentance, *teshuvah.*

The plural form *kippurim* is used to signify that there are many types of *teshuvah*, and that Hashem accepts them all if offered sincerely. As examples, there is *teshuvah tata'a and teshuvah ila'a*,[5] *teshuvah me'ahavah and teshuvah me'yirah*,[6] *teshuvah biyemei yalduto and teshuvah biyemei ziknuto*,[7] among others.

At *vidui*, some sing a victory march,[ii] while others sway intently. The Yom Kippur of the Vilna Gaon was fundamentally different from the Yom Kippur of the Ba'al Shem Tov, the Ba'al Hatanya or the Maggid of Mezeritch.

The various *kippurim* may involve elements of joy or pain, ecstasy or fear, enthusiasm or terror. All of them are valid modes of repentance.

At the conclusion of *Seliḥot*, we recount the different supplications and confessions of various individuals in the Prophets and Writings: "David, Your servant, said before You..., Ezra the Scribe said before You..., Daniel the beloved man cried out before You...." Each had a different *vidui*, a different approach to repentance. "And You gave us, Hashem our God, with love this *Yom HaKippurim*...."

---

[4] There is a well known opinion expressed by Rabbi Yehudah Hanasi maintaining that the day of Yom Kippur can effect atonement without repentance (*Yoma* 85b). However, even according to this opinion, *teshuvah* is, in fact, the *mitzvat hayom* of Yom Kippur. Man should not beg for atonement on Yom Kippur, he should claim it out of a sense of dignity, a dignity which results when atonement is not merely granted but rather earned through the act of *teshuvah.*

[5] Tanya, *Igeret Hateshuvah*, chapters 4 and 7.

[6] See *Yoma* 86b. [See also *On Repentance*, "Blotting out or Elevating Sin", for the Rav's interpretation of these terms.]

[7] Rambam, *Hilkhot Teshuvah* 2:1.

The implied lesson is that Hashem accepts various modes of repentance.

The Necessity for Global *Teshuvah*

There are numerous means to attain *kapparah* for specific transgressions; sacrifices, lashes, and the death penalty all can effect atonement. In contrast, *teshuvah* on Yom Kippur must be global. Yom Kippur is the day on which purification or *taharah* is achieved, a state that can be reached only if all sins are purged; "For through this day He will provide atonement for you, to purify you from *all* your sins before Hashem you shall be purified."

Complete purification from all sin is the condition for atonement on Yom Kippur. In this sense, the atonement of Yom Kippur is an all or nothing proposition. For this reason, Rabbi Akiva used the analogy of immersion in a mikveh to describe the purification of Yom Kippur: "Just as a mikveh purifies the impure, so (i.e. only in this way) the Holy One Blessed Be He purifies Israel" (*Yoma* 85b). If the whole body is not immersed in the mikveh waters, purification does not take place.

This same concept is implied by the language of the Rambam in his description of the necessity for *teshuvah* on Yom Kippur. When referring to the atonement process in the offering of sacrifices during the year, the Rambam states that one "must repent and confess." Yet, in describing atonement on Yom Kippur, the Rambam states, "Yom Kippur atones <u>for returnees</u> (*lashavim*)." In contrast to the atonement attained through animal sacrifice, one must be a "returnee" to attain atonement on Yom Kippur, suggesting the necessity for an all-encompassing, global *teshuvah* for all of one's misdeeds and transgressions.

There is an inherent difficulty in this requirement for global *teshuvah*. A prerequisite for atonement on individual sins is *hakarat haḥet*, recognition of the transgression that was committed. As mentioned earlier, however, *taharah* suggests total cleansing, a requirement that presumably includes sins that are unknown to us as well. Yet the three requirements of the Rambam for *vidui* (confession), namely, sin recognition, remorse, and resolution not to sin further, are precluded when there is no clear knowledge of these transgressions. How then can *taharah* take place?

According to the Rav, Hashem in His mercy grants forgiveness for sins unknown to us as well. Otherwise, the principle of *taharah* would be negated and the day of Yom Kippur could not effect atonement. The latter part of *vidui* explicitly includes confession of sins, "...that are revealed to us and those that are not revealed to us. Those that are revealed to us we have already declared before You and confessed them to You, and those that are not revealed to us are revealed and known to You."

In light of God's willingness to include unrevealed sins in the atonement of Yom Kippur, a seemingly redundant phrase in the Yom Kippur service can be understood: "And You gave us, Hashem our God, with love this *Yom HaKippurim* for pardon, forgiveness, and atonement, and to pardon all our inquities on it...." What is the purpose of the apparently superfluous phrase, "and to pardon all our iniquities..."? The answer is that "pardon, forgiveness, and atonement" are attained through an individual's *teshuvah* for sins that are known to him. The latter phrase includes sins unknown to him ("all our iniquities"), those for which *teshuvah* cannot be done.

God as Intimate: the Concept of *Meḥilah*

Of the three terms used to describe the function of Yom Kippur, "pardon, forgiveness, and atonement" (*meḥilah, seliḥah,* and *kapparah),* the latter two involve the erasure of the metaphysical aspects of sin. Only Hashem has the ability to grant *seliḥah* and *kapparah.* In contrast, under specific circumstances *meḥilah* can be granted by man to his fellow man.

For example, if one is owed a debt, it is within his power to forego collection. Through this magnanimous action one grants *mehilah* to another person, and the financial debt is cancelled.

The concept of *mehilah* goes beyond forgiveness of monetary claims. If, for example, one insults his fellow man, the person who suffers the indignity can likewise grant *mehilah*. Through this gesture, the scorned individual indicates that the indignity is no longer painful to him, and that the original act is in effect forgotten.

In the initial portion of the *kedushat hayom* blessing in the *Amidah* of Yom Kippur we request: "Our God and the God of our forefathers, pardon (*mehal*) our iniquity on this Day of Atonement." In contrast, just prior to the communal *vidui* during repetition of the *Amidah*, the phrase is slightly modified: "Our God and the God of our forefathers, <u>forgive</u> and pardon (*s'lah u'mehal*) our iniquity on this Day of Atonement."

This difference in wording can be understood in light of the dual relationship of Hashem to the Jewish people. One way in which Hashem relates to us is as absolute ruler: *Melekh al kol ha'aretz*. In this relationship, man is but a small creature in comparison to the Master of the Universe. It is in this role that God grants *selihah* and *kapparah*. When a person commits a transgression, the act has a clear metaphysical implication; the transgression defiles the individual, rendering him *tameh*, impure. To remove this consequence, a person must attain *selihah* from God, the supreme, omnipotent being.

However, the second way Hashem relates to us is as an intimate, childhood friend.[8] *Mehilah* addresses the sociological alienation between man and God as a result of sin.

_____

[8] The Rav at this point in the lecture evoked the image of two children playing ball. There are a number of Rabbinic sources which highlight this friendship. Rashi refers to Hillel's famous dictum which describes the entire message of Torah in a nutshell: "What is hateful to you, do not do to your friend." The "friend," in this case, refers to Hashem (*Shabbat* 31a).

In the body of the Yom Kippur *Amidah*, prior to the detailed *vidui* request for forgiveness of sin, we ask Hashem to "pardon (*meḥal*) our iniquities on this Yom HaKippurim." Our initial, hesitant approach to Hashem on Yom Kippur is as an estranged friend who wants to reestablish the prior intimate relationship. To convey this idea, the Rav explained that if one's son were found to be guilty of robbery, aside from the intrinsic action and its consequences, the father would in a very real sense feel betrayed by his son's deed. We don't yet ask for *seliḥah*: our concern at this point is simply that Hashem pardon us as children who have deeply disappointed their father. Only later in the prayer, as an introduction to *vidui*, are we concerned about removing the metaphysical blemish of transgression as well, and only then do we add the word *s'laḥ* to our prayer.

This reestablishment of the bond between God and man should be a reflection of the *meḥilah* we each ask of our fellow man in preparation for Yom Kippur.[9] The *piyyut* describes Yom Kippur as "a day of love and friendship, a day of abandoning jealousy and competition, a day that You will grant *meḥilah* for all our iniquities...."[iii] The inclusion of the final phrase suggests that the

---

Similarly, in the introduction to his blessing to Joseph's children (Genesis 48:15), Jacob said, "The Lord Who shepherds (*haro'eh*) me from my inception...." The Ramban in his commentary elucidates that the word *haro'eh* is derived from the word *re'a*, meaning friend (see also endnote v in the chapter on "The Message of the Shofar").

[9] In detailing the restitution one must make with his fellow man after having engaged in theft, the Rambam states that the stolen item must be returned and the thief must repent for his action. Although there is no necessity to request *meḥilah* from the owner of the stolen object at the time of restitution (*Hovel Umaẓik* 5:9), as Yom Kippur arrives one must indeed beg the aggrieved party for *meḥilah* (*Hilkhot Teshuvah* 2:9).

mehilah that God bestows us is conditioned on our granting *mehilah* to our fellow man.[10][iv]

Global *Teshuvah* and *Mehilah*

A mishnah in *Yoma* (8:9) emphasizes the importance of asking *mehilah* of our fellow man on Yom Kippur:

> Rabbi Elazar Ben Azaryah stated: For sins between man and God (*bein adam laMakom*); Yom Kippur atones; for sins between man and his fellow (*bein adam lehavero*) Yom Kippur does not atone until one appeases his fellow.

Rabbi Elazar Ben Azaryah derives this rule from the verse: "For through this day He will provide atonement for you, to purify you from all your sins [that are] before Hashem, you shall be purified." Rabbi Elazar's opinion is based on his punctuation of the verse; in his opinion a comma should be inserted after the phrase *before Hashem*, i.e., Yom Kippur atones unconditionally only for those sins that are *bein adam laMakom* or "before Hashem."[11]

A mishnah in *Bava Kamma* (8:7) echoes this theme: "Even though one has repaid [someone who he damaged], he is not pardoned until he requests forgiveness [from the injured party]." The mishnah bases this rule on a passage in Genesis 20:7, in which God tells Abimelekh that he must return Sarah to Abraham and ask forgiveness of Abraham: "But now, return the man's wife, for he is a prophet, and he will pray on your behalf."

The Rav asked why it was necessary for the mishnah to cite the Abimelekh incident to prove the halakhic requirement of asking

---

[10] As a result of this emphasis, it is clear that any arguments or personal strife that surface on Yom Kippur conflict with the entire *kedushat hayom*.

[11] In contrast, Rabbi Akiva punctuates the verse with the comma after the word *sins*: "...from all your sins, before Hashem you shall be purified."

forgiveness from an aggrieved party. Why did this mishnah not use Rabbi Elazar Ben Azaryah's proof from the phrase, "all your sins before Hashem"? [v]

The answer is that there are two implications to the requirement of asking *meḥilah* of one's fellow man. The first aspect is simply that God cannot forgive sins *bein adam leḥavero* until the sinner asks pardon from the injured. This is evident from the Abimelekh incident.

The second implication, however, has specific ramifications for Yom Kippur atonement, and it is this aspect that Rabbi Elazar Ben Azaryah emphasizes. If one has committed a transgression *bein adam leḥavero* for which he has not requested *meḥilah*, he receives no atonement at all on Yom Kippur, even for those sins that are *bein adam laMakom*. The Rav thus reads Rabbi Elazar's statement as follows: [For] sins *bein adam leḥavero* Yom Kippur does not atone [at all -- even for sins *bein adam laMakom*] until one appeases his fellow.

Why is Rabbi Elazar Ben Azaryah so strict in this requirement? Because, as explained above, unless one has engaged in *teshuvah* globally, unless one is a *shav,* the atonement is ineffective. If a person has not adequately atoned for sins *bein adam leḥavero*, he has not fulfilled the halakhic requirement of total mikveh immersion in accordance with Rabbi Akiva's analogy.

With this understanding we can attribute a second reason for the additional phrase in our request: "And You gave us, Hashem our God, with love this Yom HaKippurim for pardon, forgiveness, and atonement, and to pardon *all* our iniquities on it...." Without a complete pardon, a pardon on all iniquities including those *bein adam leḥavero*, then Yom Kippur itself is ineffective.

SHABBAT SHABBATON

The name *Shabbat Shabbaton* suggests a correspondence between Shabbat and Yom Kippur.[vi] One obvious parallel is the prohibition of proscribed work, or *melakhah*. The Gemara in *Ḥullin* 5a states that he who publicly violates the prohibitions of Shabbat is considered as one who denies the entire Torah. A halakhic implication of such public desecration is the restriction of the transgressor to act as a witness in Jewish law (*pasul la'edut*). The *Beit HaLevi* suggests that the same consequence applies to one who publicly desecrates Yom Kippur as well.

The question arises: In order for such a consequence to apply, why must the violation only be public? In fact, the Torah appears to imply that the hypocrisy underlying a sin committed in secret renders the action even more reprehensible than the same act committed in public. (Consider, for example, that the penalty for thievery is greater than the penalty for robbery.[12]) Why then is public violation of the Sabbath (and, according to the *Beit HaLevi*, violation of Yom Kippur as well) considered analogous to heresy, while private Sabbath violation does not carry the same stigma?

To answer this question, one must understand that there are three fundamental aspects to the observance of Shabbat:

1) The negative commandments regarding cessation from work
2) The positive commandments affirming the holiness of the day
3) Testimony concerning the six days of creation and the seventh day of Divine rest

It is through this third aspect that the heresy inherent in public Sabbath violation becomes evident. One who violates Shabbat

---

[12] See *Bava Kamma* 79b.

publicly denies the creation and the Creator.[13] This act of false witness occurs only when one openly violates Shabbat; violating Shabbat in private does not involve heresy, since by definition testimony is a public declaration.

However, why would public violation of Yom Kippur similarly involve this same connotation of false testimony and heresy?

Shabbat testifies to the creation of the physical world, a world of causality and time progression that is both inexorable and irreversible. The physical world is governed by quantitative rules; a stone falls according to a precise mathematical equation. This is the world in which "...day and night shall not cease" (Genesis 8:22), where the physical reality of time progression, of day and night, the sun setting and rising in a prescribed manner, is invariant. In this world, the act of *teshuvah* is an irrational gesture since it is impossible to undo the cause and effect of past events. Such a world is described in the first chapter of Genesis, a world in which the name of God as *Elokim* is used, signifying the Divine attribute of strict justice (*middat hadin*). It is God in the role of *Elokim* Who rested on the seventh day: "...and on the seventh day, *Elokim* finished His work" (Genesis 2:2).

Yom Kippur, however, testifies to a second component of creation with a different set of cosmic rules. A passage in Tractate *Nedarim* 39b states that *teshuvah* was one of seven ideas created prior to the world. The concept of *teshuvah*, whereby one can erase and even elevate previous sinful actions, suggests that there exists an alternate reality where one can transcend time and causality through the exercise of free will.[vii] This alternate world is introduced in the second chapter of Genesis, where the four letter Tetragrammaton (YKVK) is first mentioned.[viii] In contrast to *Elokim*, the Tetragrammaton invokes God as One who possesses *middat haḥesed*, the attribute of mercy. In commenting on the verse, "And it was evening and it was morning the first day (*yom*

---

13 See Rashi in *Ḥullin* 5a *s.v. alma mumar...*

eḥad)" (Genesis 1:5), the midrash states: *yom eḥad* was Yom Kippur. The message of this midrash is that without Yom Kippur and its theme of *teshuvah* as a motif, the world itself would not have been created.[ix]

Thus, through observing Shabbat, one testifies to Hashem's creation of the world of *din,* and by observing the day of Yom Kippur one testifies to Hashem's creation of the world of *ḥesed.* By publicly violating Yom Kippur one denies this second component of creation, and therefore on a halakhic level he would be considered an unfit witness just as one who denies the first component of creation through public violation of the Shabbat. Shabbat and Yom Kippur therefore complement each other, hence the use of *Shabbat Shabbaton* as an appellation for Yom Kippur.

TZOM HE'ASOR

Between Kol Nidrei and Sheheḥeyanu

At sunset on the evening of Yom Kippur, after the Kol Nidrei prayer, the *Sheheḥeyanu* blessing is recited. The blessing is timed to be completed just after sundown to coincide with the start of the holiday. During festivals this blessing is appended to the Kiddush; since there is no Kiddush on Yom Kippur, it is inserted at this point in the service.

However, between Kol Nidrei and *Sheheḥeyanu,* the following Biblical phrases are inserted:

"And it shall be forgiven *(venislaḥ)* to all the congregation of the Children of Israel, and to the stranger that dwells among them, for all the nation is in error" (Numbers 15:26).

"Please forgive *(s'laḥ na)* the iniquity of this nation according to the greatness of Your lovingkindness, and as You have forgiven this nation since Egypt until now. And Hashem said, 'I have forgiven according to your words'" (Numbers 14:19-20).

Why are these verses recited precisely at this moment in the Yom Kippur service? Furthermore, do these verses relate to Kol Nidrei or to the *Sheheḥeyanu* blessing?

Venislaḥ as the Conclusion of Kol Nidrei

Kol Nidrei is intimately associated with the concept of *hatarat nedarim*, the halakhically prescribed formula for the nullification of vows. When the Jew wishes to nullify a vow he has previously made, he may do so through *hatarat nedarim*. The central action allowing such nullification to take place is a declaration of remorse for having made the vow. In the presence of either a *beit din* or an appropriate individual he states that at the time of his utterance, had he then understood what he knows now, he never would have made the vow at all. Through the recognition that the original act was in effect a mistake, the vow is nullified retroactively. The Torah therefore provides the authority to change his intention to vow from willful to accidental on the basis of his present understanding, rather than on the basis of his state of mind at the time the vow was spoken.

Yom Kippur carries precisely the same message. Through the experience of repentance, we acknowledge that our sins were impulsive acts that do not reflect our present value system. As a result of this realization, our sins are considered as if they were committed unintentionally, even though they stemmed from a world-view whose flaws we only now recognize.

The concluding phrase of the first verse, "for all the nation is in error," thus links Kol Nidrei with the concept of *teshuvah*: sins are retroactively declared to have been committed in ignorance.

Venislaḥ and *Slaḥ Na* as the Introduction to *Sheheḥeyanu*

The experience of *simḥah* or joy is the basis for the recitation of *Sheheḥeyanu* (*Eruvin* 40b). On Yom Tov, this joy finds expression in the recitation of the *Vehasi'enu* passage during the festival *Amidah*: "Bestow upon us Hashem our God the blessing of Your festivals for life and for peace, for gladness and for joy...." Although *Vehasi'enu* is not generally recited today in the *Amidah* of Rosh Hashanah and Yom Kippur, the Rosh in his commentary near the end of Tractate *Rosh Hashanah* (*siman* 14) enumerates a number of *Ga'onim* and *Rishonim* who did in fact recite *Vehasi'enu*, thereby suggesting that this expression of joy is indeed appropriate even during the *Yamim Nora'im*.[x]

The *simḥah* of festivals is specifically associated with the eating of meat and drinking of wine (*Pesaḥim* 109a) and, in fact, *Sheheḥeyanu* is best recited over a cup of wine (*Eruvin* 40b). What then is the basis for the recitation of the blessing on Yom Kippur, when fasting is the order of the day?

The answer lies in understanding the basis for the holiday that follows Yom Kippur, the festival of Sukkot. Sukkot is in fact the holiday most clearly associated with the concept of *simḥah* (Deuteronomy 16:13-14), precisely due to its proximity to Yom Kippur. The *simḥah* of Sukkot derives from the communal forgiveness of sin that Israel experiences during Yom Kippur, the celebration of which actually takes place during Sukkot.

The *simḥah* of Yom Kippur similarly derives from this recognition. It is the communal nature of this forgiveness that is highlighted in the two verses recited prior to the *Sheheḥeyanu* blessing: "And it shall be forgiven to <u>all the congregation of the Children of Israel</u>, and to the stranger that dwells among them, for <u>all the nation</u> is in error" (Numbers 15:26). "Please forgive the iniquity of this <u>nation</u> according to the greatness of Your lovingkindness, and as You have forgiven this <u>nation</u> since Egypt until now. And Hashem said, 'I have forgiven according to your words'" (Numbers 14:19-20).

These verses deal with communal forgiveness, the forgiveness bestowed on *Knesset Yisrael*, the entire congregation of Israel as a unified entity. In contrast, another verse closely associated with Yom Kippur forgiveness: "For through this day He will provide atonement for you, to purify you from all your sins before Hashem you shall be purified" (Leviticus 16:30), would be inappropriate in this context. The verse in Leviticus deals specifically with the purification that results through the *teshuvah* of one or many individuals. Depending on the quality of such repentance, an individual or group of individuals may or may not achieve forgiveness on Yom Kippur. On the other hand, *Knesset Yisrael* gains forgiveness without fail. The *simḥah* which underlies the holiday of Yom Kippur is particularly associated with this unconditional communal forgiveness. As a result, it is specifically the verses of *venislaḥ* and *s'laḥ na* which are recited as an introduction to the *Sheheḥeyanu* blessing.

The Rav previously discussed the conceptual distinction between communal and individual confession as follows[14]:

> The difference between individual and communal confession is tremendous. When the individual confesses he does so from a state of insecurity, depression, and despair in the wake of sin. For what assurance has he that he will be acquitted of sin? And who can promise him that his transgression will be forgotten and will not haunt him till the end of his days? In contrast, *Knesset Israel* -- and each and every Jewish community is considered to be a microcosm of the whole of *Knesset Israel* -- confesses out of a sense of confidence and even rejoicing for it does so in the presence of a loyal ally, before its most beloved one. In fact, in certain communities (I myself heard this in Germany) it is

---

[14] *On Repentance*, "The Individual and the Community"

customary for the whole congregation to sing the *Al ḥet* confession in heartwarming melodies.

The individual does not sing *Al ḥet*, he weeps. Not so the community, because it does not come to plead for atonement; it claims it as its right.

The fast on Yom Kippur is referred to as *tzom he'asor* and not the more common term for a fast, *ta'anit*. The word *tzom* in another context means "braid," as used in *Mishnah Ḥullin* 4:6 through the term *tzomet hagiddin* or braided sinews. A braid is a collection of individual strands unified into a single entity. On Yom Kippur we celebrate the forgiveness of sin bestowed on *Knesset Yisrael* as a *gavra,* a communal "personality" which transcends a collection of individuals. This joyful recognition is thus the basis for reciting the *Sheheḥeyanu* blessing which allows us to thank Hashem "...Who has kept us alive, sustained us, and brought us to this time."

NOTES

[i] In his summer *Yarḥei Kallah* lecture of 1971 (summarized in *Nora'ot Harav,* Volume 6), the Rav dedicated three days to discussing the various aspects of the *kedushah* of Yom Kippur. The lectures were based on a disagreement that the Rav perceived between Reb Elazar Hakallir, who made use of these three appellations for Yom Kippur, and the Rambam, who made use of only two: *Shvitat Asor* and *Yom Kippurim.* According to the Rav, the Rambam combined two of Hakallir's categories of *Tzom He'asor* and *Shabbat Shabbaton* into one: *Shvitat Asor.* The halakhic implications of these two categories are discussed in endnote vi below.

[ii] See *On Repentance,* "The Individual and the Community", where the Rav describes *vidui* in southern Germany.

[iii] See:

מסורה, חוברת ב, תשרי תש'ן ("מפי השמועה ממרן הגרי"ד סולוביצ'יק")
<u>בענין אין יוה"כ מכפר עד שירצה את חבירו:</u>
אין יוה"כ מכפר עד שירצה את חבירו, וזה דין נוסף על החובה דכל השנה שחייב לבקש ממנו מחילה, דבעד כפרת יוה"כ לא די בזה שחתברו מחלו אלא דצריך גם לרצות את חברו, כלומר, שיחזיר ויהפוך את המצב לכמות שהיה קודם שחטא לו, ויחזור היחס של חברות ורעות שהיה שרוי ביניהם קודם שחטא לו. ובטעמא דמילתא נראה לומר, דכפרת יוה"כ באה בתורת <i>כפרת הציבור</i>, ואין היחיד מתכפר אלא <i>דרך הציבור</i>, שהרי שעיר המשתלח קרבן ציבור הוא, וא"כ בכדי לצרף ולאחד את הציבור יחד צריך שלא תהא שום מחיצה המבדילה בין אנשי הציבור. וזהו שיסד הפייטן בסוף סדר העבודה "יום שימת אהבה ורעות".

[iv] There is a difference in nuance in the Rav's explanation of *meḥilah* as it appears in *On Repentance,* "Expiation, Suffering and Redemption":

> Pardon (*meḥilah*) is a concept that does not pertain only to sin and to the Day of Atonement. It is a juridical concept and has application in the area of civil law as well. When a man is in debt to a friend who "excuses" him by waiving repayment of all or part of his debt, then the debtor is released from the bondage of obligation under which he labored until that act of pardon (*meḥilah*). Such is the case regarding the pardon

that is conferred by the Day of Atonement. A man transgresses incurring
guilt; and the Day of Atonement affords him a remission of sentence.

In this passage, the Rav's emphasis is on relief of the debt one owes God
for having transgressed, as opposed to reestablishing a relationship that had
become strained.

ᵛ See *Halakhic Positions of Rabbi Joseph B. Soloveitchik,* p. 162, where
the Rav is cited as providing another answer to this question: "In all year-
round confrontations, merely pacifying a friend is sufficient. This is what
the mishnah in Bava Kamma states. However, before Yom Kippur,
ordinary appeasement is not enough. We are required to seek a restored
relationship, to enjoy the kind of deep and trusting friendship we enjoyed
before the misunderstanding occurred."

ᵛⁱ According to the Rambam, who uses *Shvitat He'asor* as the second
aspect of the holiness of Yom Kippur (see endnote i above), this term
includes both the fasting and resting imperatives of Yom Kippur.
According to the Rav, there is a practical implication to the combined
kedushah suggested by this term, as follows:

The designated individual (the *ish iti*) who led *the sa'ir hamishtalei'ah*
through the desert was offered food and drink at each of ten huts that he
passed enroute. According to the Rambam (*Avodat Yom HaKippurim* 3:7):
"If his strength fails him, and he requires food [in order to continue his
mission], he may eat." The permissibility of eating on Yom Kippur to
complete the *sa'ir hamishtalei'ah* ritual as indicated by the Rambam
would, however, seem problematic. Although there is no prohibition, and
indeed a requirement to engage in the specific acts of work (*melakhah*)
necessary to offer the public sacrifices on Yom Kippur, by what right could
the *ish iti* violate the prohibition against eating on Yom Kippur? The
answer lies in the fact that the one term *shvitat asor* encompasses both the
prohibitions of *melakhah* and eating; just as *melakhah* is permissible for
the sake of public sacrifice, so too is eating. In contrast, based on his
separate categorizations of *Shabbat Shabbaton* and *Tzom He'asor*, the Rav
suggested that Rabbi Elazar Hakallir would hold that the prohibitions
against working and eating are entirely unrelated. He would therefore
maintain that although food and drink was extended to the *ish iti*, the offer

must be refused. Refreshment was offered merely to help alleviate the *ish iti's* possible anxiety that food was not available: אינו דומה מי שיש לו פת בסלו למי שאינו- (כתובות סג.)

vii See *Halakhic Man*, pp.113-15:

> Halakhic man is engaged in self-creation, in creating a new "I." He does not regret an irretrievably lost past but a past still in existence, one that stretches into and interpenetrates with the present and the future...There is a past and there is a future that are connected with one another and with the present only through the law of causality --the cause found at moment A links up with the effect taking place at moment B, and so on. However, time itself as past appears only as "no more" and as future appears as "not yet.". From this perspective repentance is an empty and hollow concept. It is impossible to regret a past that is already dead, lost in the abyss of oblivion...However, there is a past which persists in its existence...a past [which] enters into the domain of the present and links up with the future...past, present, and future merge and blend together, and this threefold time structure arises before us adorned with a splendid unity... We do not have here the determinate order of a scientific, causal process...The future imprints its stamp on the past and determines its image....
>
> The main principle of repentance is that the future dominates the past and there reign over it in unbounded fashion. Sin, as a cause and as the beginning of a lengthy causal chain of destructive acts, can be transformed, underneath the guiding hand of the future, into a source of merit and good deeds, into love and fear of God. The cause is located in the past, but the direction of its development is determined by the future. Great is repentance, for deliberate sins are accounted to him as meritorious deeds [Yoma 86b]...In this outlook we find contained the basic principle of choice and free will...If a causal lawfulness molds man's spiritual personality and points the way wherein he must go, then self-creation can have no meaning...To be sure, each cause gives rise to a new causal sequence. But this sequence can oftentimes head

in various directions...If man so desires, it will travel in the direction of eternity; the past will heed his word and attach itself to him.

For a detailed analysis of the Rav's thoughts on the relationship between repentance and time, see the chapter entitled: תשובה וזמן בהגות הרב, by Eliezer Goldman in סולובייצ'יק, אמונה בזמנים משתנים.

[viii] Although only implied in this *derashah*, this concept of non-physical time is connoted by the Tetragrammaton because of the merging of *haya, hoveh and yih'yeh*, past, present and future. The initial repetition of the Tetragrammaton in the Thirteen Attributes of Mercy is interpreted by the Gemara precisely with this conception of time in mind: "I am YKVK before man sins, and I am YKVK after man sins and repents" (*Rosh Hashanah* 17b). Despite having engaged in actions which distance man from G-d, the sublime relationship of G-d to the penitent is reestablished, often even strengthened (as in *teshuvah me'ahavah*). The very efficacy of *teshuvah* is thus based on this metaphysical concept of time.

[ix] The midrash itself reads as follows: "*'Vayehi erev'* (and it was evening) -- these are the actions of the wicked; *'vayehi voker'* (and it was morning) -- these are the actions of the righteous, *'yom ehad'* -- that the Holy One Blessed Be He gave them one day. Which [day]? Yom HaKippurim" (*Bereishit Rabbah* 3:8). The midrash here is not suggesting that the first day of creation was Yom Kippur, since it is Rosh Hashanah that is associated with creation.

[x] A discussion regarding the history of *Vehasi'enu* in this context appears in כבוד הרב, in Dr. Sherman's essay, שמחת יום טוב ושמחת ראש השנה.

The Day of Yom Kippur as the Medium for Atonement[*]

There is a uniqueness to the day of Yom Kippur which separates it from any other day of the year, in that the day itself is invested with the power to provide atonement. The Ḥayyei Adam, in the *Tefillah Zakkah* meditation (the introductory Yom Kippur prayer read prior to Kol Nidrei), refers to the day of Yom Kippur as "a singular day in the year...a 'powerful' day in the year." Assigning such a profound capability to a period of time (the "*itzumo shel yom*") was mentioned by the Rav on numerous occasions as a most sublime mystery. Yet because of the centrality of this theme, the Rav raised this topic in virtually every one of his *teshuvah derashot*.

---

[*] BASED ON THE 1973 AND 1976 *TESHUVAH DERASHOT*

INVOKING THE HOLINESS OF YOM KIPPUR

There is an anomalous view, formulated by the *Tanna* known as Rebbe (Rabbi Yehudah Hanasi) that the day of Yom Kippur provides atonement even if the individual does not engage in *teshuvah* (*Shevuot* 13a). The Rav, in clarifying this difficult opinion, had discussed Rebbe's ruling in earlier *teshuvah* lectures.[i] In his 1976 *Teshuvah Derashah* the Rav clarified a specific detail discussed by Rashi regarding Rebbe's view -- a detail that cuts to the very essence of Yom Kippur.

Rebbe states that atonement is bestowed to all on Yom Kippur, even if an individual ignores the most basic of Yom Kippur obligations. Among these violated imperatives, Rebbe lists not fasting, not abstaining from work, and "[not] declaring (the day of Yom Kippur) as a holy convocation." Rashi, in explaining Rebbe's opinion, clarifies that the failure to make this declaration means: "The person did not say the blessing [which appears towards the end of each Yom Kippur *Amidah*]: '[He Who] sanctifies Israel and Yom HaKippurim.' "

Tosafot strongly disagree with Rashi's interpretation of "[not] declaring (the day of Yom Kippur) as a holy convocation." *Tosafot* argues that Rebbe must obviously be discussing a very major violation if he groups this latter transgression together with eating and working. Yet, the requirement for expressing such a blessing in the *Amidah* is not even Biblically mandated; how could Rashi possibly group such a relatively minor infraction with the far more severe violations of eating and working?

According to the Rav, Rashi's interpretation can be explained through an understanding of the *Kohen Gadol*'s *vidui* on Yom Kippur. The *Kohen Gadol*'s *vidui* reads, in part, "Please, through Your Name, Hashem, forgive the errors, iniquities, and sins..." (*Mishnah Yoma* 6:2). This version of *vidui* includes two fundamental components: recognition of sin and request for forgiveness. In contrast, our *vidui* of today involves remorse and resolve, with no request for forgiveness. The request for forgiveness in our contemporary prayers does not appear in *vidui* itself, but rather appears in the concluding paragraph of the *Amidah* prayer prior to *vidui*. In this paragraph, the holiness of Yom Kippur (the *kedushat hayom*) is the main theme: "Our God and God of our fathers, pardon our iniquities on this day of Yom Kippur." Why does the request for forgiveness precede the formal *vidui*, and not appear in *vidui* itself,[1] in contrast to the *vidui* of the *Kohen Gadol*?

The placement of the request for forgiveness within the blessing of the *kedushat hayom* is most pertinent. The request for forgiveness does not originate in a vacuum, but is connected to the day of Yom Kippur and the atonement that the day affords. Although a simple request for atonement can be made any time during the year, the specific request for atonement through the day of Yom Kippur can only be made on Yom Kippur. Therefore, the request for atonement appears specifically within the blessing associated with the *kedushat hayom.*

The complete *vidui* of the *Kohen Gadol* reflects this emphasis: "Please, through Your Name, Hashem,[2,ii] forgive the errors, inquities, and sins...as it is written in the Torah of Your servant Moshe: For through this day He will atone for you, to purify you, from all your sins before Hashem you will be purified" (*Mishnah Yoma* 6:2). Why is it necessary for the *Kohen Gadol* to "remind" Hashem that it is Yom Kippur? Because the *Kohen Gadol* must request the specific atonement that is bestowed upon us through the day of Yom Kippur.

The statement, "pardon our iniquities on this *Yom HaKippurim*" within our *Amidah* prayer, thus parallels that of the

---

[1] The statement ...ועל כולם אלוק סליחות סלח לנו within the body of על חטא is a later insertion by the liturgist, and is not an intrinsic part of *vidui*.

[2] This is the version of the mishnah in the *Yerushalmi* as quoted in Tosafot on Yoma 35b, the version that appears in our own present-day *Avodah* recitation.

Kohen Gadol: "Please, through Your Name, Hashem, forgive the errors, inquities, and sins....for through this day He will atone for you..." We mention Yom Kippur as the very basis for the atonement request. In this blessing we cite three Biblical verses to buttress our request:

> Our God and the God of our forefathers, pardon our iniquities on this Yom Kippur. Wipe away and remove our sins and iniquities from before Your eyes, as it is said: "I, only I, am the one Who wipes away your sins for My sake, and I will not recall your iniquities" (Isaiah 43:25), and it is [also] said: "I have wiped away your iniquities like a cloud and your sins like a mist -- return to Me for I have redeemed you"(Isaiah 44:22), and it is [also] said: "For through this day He will atone for you, to purify you, from all your sins before Hashem you shall be purified" (Leviticus 16:30).

The final verse ("For through this day...") is needed because merely requesting forgiveness is insufficient: one must ask for forgiveness through the day of of Yom Kippur. As a result, a specific verse must be used in which the day of Yom Kippur is invoked in this context.

We can now return to the original difficulty in Rashi's interpretation of Rebbe's statement. According to Rashi, the invocation of the *kedushat hayom* is not merely a Rabbinic ordinance. Since, according to Rebbe's assertion, it is the day of Yom Kippur that effects atonement even without *teshuvah,* one might naturally think at the very least that there must be a requirement to invoke the *kedushat hayom* in order to experience this atonement. According to Rashi's interpretation of Rebbe's statement, however, Rebbe obviates this assumption by indicating that he is of the opinion that not even this invocation itself is a requirement to gain atonement.

As a result, according to the opinion that differs with Rebbe's (the normative halakhic opinion that *teshuvah* is indeed necessary to receive atonement on Yom Kippur), one can infer that there is in fact a requirement for such a specific appeal during the Yom Kippur service. In fact, this requirement is evident not only in the *kedushat hayom* blessing of the *Amidah*, but in the prayer immediately following the *Amidah* of *Ma'ariv,* as the Rav subsequently clarified.

As explained in the previous chapter on the *Seliḥot* service, the collection of *Seliḥot* supplications commences with the prayer called *Shome'a Tefillah,* "Hearer of prayer." The theme of *Shome'a Tefillah* is the proclamation of God as the King of the Cosmos as well as of Israel. The function of *Shome'a Tefillah* as an introduction to *Seliḥot* is based on the rule: "A person should first praise the Holy One Blessed Be He and then pray" (*Berakhot* 32b). Only after reciting this collection of verses do we reach the body of the *Seliḥot,* that contains at its core the Thirteen Attributes of Mercy. In *Seliḥot,* we make numerous requests: for the forgiveness of sin, the rebuilding of the Temple and Jerusalem, as well as for private needs. Prior to making requests of Hashem one must first glorify Him.

Yet, on Yom Kippur night, immediately after the *Amidah,* just as we are about to recite *Seliḥot,* there is an intervening *piyyut* recited even prior to *Shome'a Tefillah* called *Ya'aleh.* Why does this prayer appear precisely at this point in the service?[3]

As we conclude the *Amidah* prayer of Yom Kippur night, we are poised to recite the special *Seliḥot* of Yom Kippur, consisting of repeated requests for atonement. As explained earlier, in order for us to attain the atonement bestowed on Yom Kippur, this request must contain the element of *kedushat hayom.* We do not ask for the atonement accessible on any other day; we request the specific atonement of Yom Kippur. Yet, if one examines the wording of any

---

[3] The Rav interjected that while growing up in his father's house, he learned that the Yom Kippur prayer book is a text which must be studied with the same depth as the most involved Talmudic *sugya.*

of these supplications, Yom Kippur is not even mentioned. Instead, it is within the prayer of *Ya'aleh* wherein we ask that all the prayers of that evening and the next day until nightfall be offered within the overall context of the *kedushat hayom.*

From the very first stanza of *Ya'aleh*, the theme becomes evident: "May our supplication rise from evening, and let our cry come from morning, and may our prayer be seen from evening." The repeated use of the preposition "from" would seem to be out of place here. A less stilted rendering might have read, "May our supplication rise *in* the evening..." Yet, in light of the above explanation, use of the preposition "from" is in fact most appropriate. Through this prayer we are requesting that our supplications rise as a result of (or "from") the *kedushat hayom* experienced in the evening, and so on. The prayer *Ya'aleh* is therefore not so much a prayer as it is a declaration that we wish to couple all our varied requests for atonement and forgiveness on Yom Kippur with the transcendent *kedushat hayom.*

At this point, let us step back and ask: Why it is so critical that our request for forgiveness be coupled with the concept of the *kedushat hayom*? Additionally the phrase used by the Rambam is: "The *itzumo shel yom* atones" -- what precisely does *itzumo shel yom* mean?

The word *itzumo* means "strength." The potency of the day is subjective, directly proportional to the feeling of the Jew on Yom Kippur. To some, the *itzumo shel yom* can indeed be great and powerful. Its sheer greatness has the capability of shocking and traumatizing the individual; he feels as though he is standing directly in front of an all-embracing God. Yet, for others, the *itzumo shel yom* is almost nonexistent. Yom Kippur prayer continually invokes the *kedushat hayom* so we are prompted to feel the *itzumo shel yom*. If one internalizes the truly awesome power of the day, he emerges from Yom Kippur a different person.

In this vein, the Rav cited his seminal work *Halakhic Man*, in which he described a childhood scene on the afternoon of Yom Kippur in this way:[4]

> I remember how once, on the Day of Atonement, I went outside into the synagogue courtyard with my father [R. Moses Soloveitchik], just before the Ne'ilah service. It had been a fresh, clear day, one of the fine, almost delicate days of summer's end, filled with sunshine and light. Evening was fast approaching and an exquisite autumn sun was sinking in the west, beyond the trees of the cemetery, into a sea of purple and gold. R. Moses, a halakhic man par excellence, turned to me and said: "This sunset differs from ordinary sunsets for with it forgiveness is bestowed upon us for our sins" (the end of the day atones.)[iii] The Day of Atonement and the forgiveness of sin merged and blended here with the splendor and beauty of the world and with the hidden lawfulness of the order of creation and the whole was transformed into one living, holy, cosmic phenomenon.

Rav Moshe Soloveitchik's entire being was interwoven with an appreciation of the profound significance of this particular sunset. When the consciousness is this powerful, the *itzumo shel yom* is indeed potent and the resulting atonement is all the more effective.

Invoking the *kedushat hayom* is not as important as experiencing the *itzumo shel yom*, and feeling the warm embrace of Hashem. The atonement one receives through the *itzumo shel yom* is directly proportional to the closeness one feels towards Hashem. Through this experience the penitent provides "power" to the day.

---

[4] *Halakhic Man*, p. 38.

THE BLESSING OF *KEDUSHAT HAYOM*

The blessing in the *Amidah* that pertains to *kedushat hayom* on
Rosh Hashanah starts as follows:

> Our God and God of our fathers, rule over the entire world in
> Your glory, and rise up over the entire world in Your grandeur....
> sanctify us with Your mitzvot and give us our portion in Your
> Torah.

There are two themes introduced here: God's sovereignty over
the world and the holiness of the day. However, in the *Amidah*
blessing of Yom Kippur the first theme is changed:

> Our God and God of our fathers, pardon our iniquities on this
> Yom Kippur... sanctify us with Your mitzvot and give us our
> portion in your Torah.

Here, the aspect of God's sovereignty is replaced by a request
for forgiveness. Yet, in the conclusion of this blessing we state:

> Blessed are You, Hashem, the King, Who pardons our iniquities
> and the iniquities of the entire House of Israel, and removes our
> trespasses every single year, King over all the world, Who
> sanctifies Israel and Yom Kippur.

The theme of God's sovereignty reappears. If on Yom Kippur
the theme was omitted from the introduction (called the *tofet*), why
does it appear in the conclusion (the *ḥatimah*)?[5]

---

[5] Note that the Rambam, in his siddur, indeed maintained the sovereignty
theme in the *tofet haberakhah* in his version of the prayer using the same
wording as on Rosh Hashanah. The Tur (או"ח סי' תריט) discusses a
difference of opinion on this matter. The Rambam's opinion only begs the
question, however: Why is this theme omitted in our version?

The key to understanding this apparent anomaly in the prayer service of Yom Kippur lies in a passage from the Ramban's commentary.[6] According to the Ramban, Rosh Hashanah is associated with Hashem's attribute of strict justice, *middat hadin*, to which the theme of God's sovereignty has a close connection. Nature exists according to rules that are fixed and immutable. These rules of nature are reflected in similarly immutable rules regarding punishment as a consequence of sin. On Rosh Hashanah, when Hashem is manifest to the world as King, the world is judged and found wanting, guilty. On the simple basis of *din*, we have no chance for survival.

Yet the Ramban also states that "Rosh Hashanah is a day of judgment in mercy, and Yom Kippur is a day of mercy in judgment." The shofar which is sounded on Rosh Hashanah pleads for amnesty on our behalf. Mankind is indeed found guilty, but on Rosh Hashanah Hashem allows us to continue to live. The King is a ruler but He also grants favor. This is the meaning of "justice in mercy": initially we are judged and found wanting, but the sentence is suspended. Despite this suspension, however, the sentence remains. Therefore, as the Ramban outlined, Rosh Hashanah is a day of strict judgment that ends in mercy.

In contrast, Yom Kippur represents "mercy in judgment." Hashem does not render His verdict as a monarch, but as a father.[7] A father does not generally render strict judgment on a son.[8] On Yom Kippur, we emerge victorious in judgment, because mercy is

---

[6] Ramban on Leviticus 23:24.

[7] This is the point of Rabbi Akiva's use of the term, "your Father in Heaven" (ואביכם שבשמים) in his homily. In contrast, on Rosh Hashanah our approach to Hashem is in doubt, as is evident from our equivocation in the liturgical portrayal of our relationship: אם כבנים, אם כעבדים -- possibly as sons, possibly as slaves.

[8] That is, unless he falls into the category of a "rebellious son" (Deuteronomy 21:18).

an intrinsic part of the judgment. On Yom Kippur we are pardoned -- our sentence is entirely removed.

The *tofet* part of the paragraph in the *Amidah* dealing with *kedushat hayom* performs the function of a request. Because of the father-son relationship of Hashem to His people on Yom Kippur, a request that He act as King ("rule over the whole world in Your majesty") would be entirely inappropriate. We do not want Him to assert Himself as King and thereby hand down a strict verdict. However, the theme of sovereignty is indeed mentioned in the concluding *hatimah* section, because this portion of the blessing is not a request but a description. In the conclusion of the blessing, the sovereignty theme does indeed appear ("Blessed are You Hashem...a King Who pardons and forgives our sins...") because any objective description of God must of necessity mention God as Sovereign. Yet, even here we temper the description to include the fact that He also forgives sin. This is the meaning of the phrase used by the Ramban, "mercy in judgment."

APPROACHING HASHEM

In discussing the *teshuvah* imperative the prophet Hosea states: "Return O Israel until Hashem [*ad Hashem*] for you have stumbled in your iniquity" (Hosea 14:2). There is a significant difference between the phrases "until [*ad*] Hashem" and "to [*el*] Hashem." The latter would suggest a return to the ways of Hashem. *Ad Hashem*, in contrast, means approaching Hashem himself. One who repents must not only strive to do mitzvot, but he must literally pine for Hashem. The Rav expressed the opinion that although the aspect of *el Hashem* is evident in the American religious community, the experience of *ad Hashem* is sorely lacking.

To better illustrate this point, the Rav continued by suggesting that Judaism rests on three attributes of the individual, signified by the head, the hand, and the heart.

The head involves the intellectual discipline inherent in Judaism. An ignoramus cannot be a good Jew. The ideal of *talmud Torah* involves the highest levels of logic, the ability to think abstractly, analytically, and conceptually. The rigor of Torah learning is equivalent to, and perhaps surpasses, the most modern of philosophical methods. The learning of Torah is therefore nothing less than the sanctification of the mind through intellectual struggle.

The hand involves mitzvah performance. In this respect, many *ba'alei teshuvah* excel, being vigilant to keep those mitzvot that are difficult as well as those that are easy -- all with precision. Through such performance, a person's hands are sanctified.

Although one can find the first two attributes in abundance today, it is the third aspect which the Rav has found wanting among contemporary Jews. The heart involves experiencing God emotionally. "God desires the heart" (*Sanhedrin* 106b). One must feel the emotional pull of the *Ribono Shel Olam* or, as William James put it, "the presence of the Unseen." [iv]

Can a Jew genuinely feel His presence? The Rav said that based on his own personal experience, the encounter with God is eminently possible. Man not only must believe in Hashem; he must feel God's hand supporting his head during times of emotional turmoil. Potential *ba'alei teshuvah* pine for the sublime sense of hearing Hashem's whisper. The experience of *ad Hashem* involves the very real perception of contact, communication, and dialogue. This sensation is expressed in a passage in *Tractate Yoma*: "Great is *teshuvah* for it allows one to approach the Heavenly throne" (*Yoma* 86a).

In his lecture of 1973, the Rav indicated that without this feeling of the presence of Hashem six years earlier, when he suffered the loss of his mother, brother, and especially his wife, all in the same year, he would not have been able to maintain his emotional equilibrium. The perception of God's proximity was particularly strong during the study of Torah; while poring over the opinions of Abaye and Rava, the Rav stated that he sensed the presence of Hashem with him in the room. The command of "cleaving to Him" is an imperative that can only be realized when one feels His presence and stands *lifnei Hashem.*

NOTES

[i] See *On Repentance*, "The Individual and the Community".

[ii] The Rav emphasized that the word here is בשם and not השם. The "ב" used here is an instrumental preposition, indicating that the *Kohen Gadol* was requesting atonement through the Name of Hashem [it is important to note that the *Bavli* does not contain the "ב" in the version of the *Kohen Gadol*'s *vidui*, but merely repeats the name of Hashem: אנא ה' כפר נא]. The version that includes the preposition is found in the *Yerushalmi*, and is cited by *Tosafot* as an alternate reading of the *vidui* in *Yoma* 35b. The very same use of the preposition is emphasized in the phrase כי ביום הזה יכפר עליכם: our request is that the day of Yom Kippur be the atonement medium.

 While discussing the parallel use of the preposition in these two contexts, the Rav made the following somewhat enigmatic statement in his 1979 *derashah*: "If the Name of Hashem provides כפרה and the day of Yom Kippur also provides כפרה, then it would therefore seem that the two are equivalent. It is interesting to note that [for this reason] the gedolei Hasidim never used the appellation 'Yom Kippur'; they referred to the day as *Yom Hakadosh*." (See פרק טז as cited in בני יששכר חודש תשרי מאמר ח ש.י. עגנון , ימים נוראים, for more detail regarding this custom.)

 In the 1979 *teshuvah derashah*, the Rav continued to explain that there were three השתחויות performed during the *Avodah*, all in response to the שם המפורש. However, the שם המפורש was not only invoked on Yom Kippur, it was also said every day at ברכת כהנים . Why is there no bowing during the יציאת שם המפרש in ברכת כהנים? Bowing is done only when the Name of Hashem is said בתורת מכפר. Therefore, in the *Nusaḥ Ashkenaz* version of the *Avodah*, there is no bowing at the time that the *Kohen* declares לה' חטאת over the שעיר 'לה; the use of the שם ה', in this case is only for identification purposes. [However, in the *Nusaḥ Sefard* version of the *Avodah*, אתה כוננת, there is indeed an additional bow at the declaration of לה'חטאת. According to this שיטה, the declaration of the שם ה'

is also part of the כפרה. Similarly, ברכת כהנים requires no bowing, since this blessing has no aspect of כפרה.]

With regard to the bowing itself, in the *Beit Hamikdash* the halakhah was that one's face had to be against the floor, an action which is only done on Yom Kippur, and only in response to the שם המפורש. Only those in the עזרה would bow; those outside (in the עזרת נשים) did not bow; they only responded ברוך שם כבוד מלכותו לעולם ועד. Today, bowing during the *Avodah* recitation is only a custom. It is interesting to note that the Vilna Gaon and other Lithuanian gedolim did not allow the שליח ציבור to bow at all, since not only is he prohibited from being מעקר רגליו during חזרת הש"ץ, but the שליח ציבור must constantly maintain his erect posture.

[iii] In the context of the previous discussion, it is appropriate to cite the footnote (42) of the Rav on this statement in *Halakhic Man*:

> See *Shevu'ot* 13b: "If a person ate a piece of meat [on the Day of Atonement] and choked on it until he died" [even Rabbi who says that the Day of Atonement atones for sins committed on the day itself would admit that the sinner in this instance would incur *karet*, would be cut off]. *Tosafot,* ad loc., states: The Talmud does not necessarily mean that the person must have choked on the meat [in order not to receive atonement], for the same law would apply as long as the person [who ate the meat] died before the end of the day atones. Thus, the Tosafists are of the opinion that the end of the day atones. [Therefore, if the person died before the end of the day, he does not receive atonement for his sin.] Rashi, however, states: "He committed his sin [until his death] so that not even one moment of the day elapsed after his sin." His view is that the entire day atones. [Therefore, if even one moment of the day elapsed from the time the person committed the sin of eating until his death, that moment would bestow atonement for his sin.] See Rashba, ad. loc.

[iv] See the published lecture by William James: "The Reality of the Unseen," in *The Varieties of Religious Experience* (New York: Random House, 1902), 53-76. The lecture consists largely of anecdotal information detailing subjective religious experiences, maintaining that "It is as if there

were in the human consciousness a sense of reality, a feeling of objective presence, a perception of what we might call 'something there,' more deep and more general than any of the special and particular 'senses' by which the current psychology supposes existent realities to be originally revealed."

The *Avodah* Recitation and The Conclusion of Yom Kippur*

THE *AVODAH*

The Temple service on Yom Kippur (the *Avodah*) was always an area of intense interest to the Rav. The intricate detail of the *Avodah* was the topic of a *Yarḥei Kallah*, a series of three all-day lectures, taught by the Rav in the summer of 1971, as well as the primary topic in one of his last *Kinus Teshuvah* lectures given to the Rabbinical Council in 1979.

In large part, the Rav's focus on the *Avodah* was clearly connected to his sheer mastery of the subject matter; the Rav had a long tradition of staying awake every Yom Kippur night to study the *Avodah* ritual in detail with his father, Rabbi Moshe Soloveitchik *zt"l*. On a philosophical level, the Rav's interest in

---

* BASED ON THE 1973, 1976 AND 1979 *TESHUVAH DERASHOT*. A portion of this chapter was previously published in *Jewish Action*, September 1994.

this subject may have been related to his abiding interest in the
subject of holiness, an underlying theme in much of his writing.
Holiness is defined by the Rav in *Halakhic Man* as "the descent of
divinity into the midst of our concrete world." The encounter
between finitude and infinity was most closely realized at the
pinnacle of the *Avodah* ritual, the moment that the High Priest
entered the Holy of Holies. Finally, on a simply personal level, the
Rav related:

> *As a child, I keenly felt the* kedushas hayom *of Yom Kippur.
> The holiness of Yom Kippur was not merely a phrase; it
> was an experience I do not know how to adequately relate.
> The enthusiasm, the ecstasy, the recognition of this holiness
> reached its pinnacle at the* Avodah.

The Rav was, of course, referring to the long interlude during
the *Musaf Amidah* when the cantor and congregation recite the
various *piyyutim* which describe the Yom Kippur *Avodah* ritual as
it was practiced in the era of the Temple's existence. The *Otzar
Hagaonim* states that in many congregations this *Avodah* on Yom
Kippur was recited not only during the repetition of the *Musaf
Amidah*, but during *Shaharit* and *Minhah* as well. Although the
gaonim later annulled the custom of these multiple recitations,
when Rav Hai Gaon was *dayan* of Baghdad the *Avodah* was recited
during both the *Shaharit* and *Musaf* repetitions of the *Amidah*. This
custom of multiple recitations suggests a special attraction that
early Rabbinic luminaries had for this particular portion of the Yom
Kippur service, an attraction which, as illustrated above, was
clearly shared by the Rav himself.

The *Avodah* recitation itself is mentioned only once in the
Gemara, in a brief reference in *Yoma* 36b. Rashi there states one
reason for this recitation: the *Avodah* was recited in order to fulfill
the verse, *u'neshalmah parim sefateinu* – "and we will offer
[instead of sacrifices] the calves of our lips" (Hosea 14:3).

To clarify this imperative, the Rav quoted a Gemara in *Megillah* 31b that recounts a conversation between Hashem and Abraham in the context of the *brit bein habetarim,* the "covenant between the pieces" (Genesis 15). Abraham asked how he was to know that God would not forsake Israel if they sinned. Hashem answered, "in the merit of the [Temple] sacrifices." Abraham insisted that this merit is fine when these sacrifices are in existence, but what was to happen after the destruction of the Temple? Hashem replied that if the Children of Israel learned the laws surrounding the sacrifices, he would consider their study as a virtual sacrificial offering. When we cannot offer sacrifices, we recite the halakhot pertaining to them as a substitute. *U'neshalmah parim sefateinu* refers to the present-day mitzvah of reciting the details of various sacrifices at precisely those times of year that they would normally be offered in the Temple. The Rashi above therefore suggests that the *Avodah* recited in *Musaf* is a fulfillment of the same mitzvah.

Although *u'neshalmah parim sefateinu* would initially seem to be a compelling rationale behind our present-day recitation of the *Avodah* ritual, the Rav explained that this phrase alone is insufficient to explain many of the customs and laws surrounding this recitation. For example, immediately prior to the *Avodah* the cantor chants *Oḥilah laKel*, a special supplication for the cantor, as representative of the community, to be given Divine assistance in leading the service that is to follow. Why does the cantor need this introductory prayer specifically before leading the *Avodah* service on Yom Kippur? Why is it not recited before the sacrifice detail in every other *Musaf* prayer throughout the year?[1]

---

[1] On the Shabbat prior to Passover, the cantor recites a similar introductory *piyyut (Avo beḥayil)*, prior to a *piyyut* which details the halakhot of *ḥametz* and matzah. However, in this case the *ḥazan* is asking permission to detail halakhot which are applicable today. In contrast, the *Avodah* in our day is not in practice.

Moreover, a recitation of the *Avodah* detail actually took place in the course of the *Avodah* ritual itself, as performed in the Temple. At the point at which the *Kohen Gadol* dispatched the *sa'ir hamishtalei'aḥ*, the *Kohen Gadol* publicly read to all those assembled in the Temple courtyard (according to Rashi) the three sections in the Torah which discuss the Yom Kippur *Avodah* ritual and the halakhot associated with Yom Kippur. The function of this public reading was clearly unrelated to *u'neshalmah parim sefateinu* since the *Beit Hamikdash* was obviously still in existence. Yet this part of the service was so important that without it the whole *Avodah* was rendered invalid.

Clearly then, there must be a significance to the *Avodah* recitation beyond a simple fulfillment of *u'neshalmah parim sefateinu.*

An Affirmation of *Torah Sheb'al Peh*

In the time of Ezra the Scribe, a translator (*meturgaman*) was employed during the public Torah readings throughout the year in order to explicate its content in harmony with *Torah Sheb'al Peh*, the oral law. However, according to the Rav, a unique aspect of the *Kohen Gadol*'s public reading was the absence of such a *meturgaman*; the *Kohen Gadol* himself expounded *Torah Sheb'al Peh* as he read from the Torah.

The critical importance of the *Torah Sheb'al Peh* exposition of *Torah Shebikhtav* (the written law) in this public reading on Yom Kippur, and the fact that the *Kohen Gadol* himself had to make these clarifications, can be understood in light of a dramatic inconsistency between the literal description of the *Avodah* in *Torah Shebikhtav* and its actual practice in the *Beit Hamikdash.*

First, the Rav explained that the description of the *Avodah* in Leviticus 16 is complete in almost every way. One seldom finds any Biblically mandated mitzvah formulated in this amount of detail. However, there is one anomaly in the Biblical prescription. In the course of the *Avodah* description, at the point in which the scapegoat is dispatched to the desert, the Torah states: "And Aaron came to the Tent of Meeting and removed the linen garments…" (Leviticus 16:23). According to the Gemara in *Yoma* 71a, this portion of the ritual is out of sequence. The change of garments actually took place much later in the *Avodah*: after the removal of the *kaf u'mahtah*, the incense ladle and shovel, from the Holy of Holies. The reason for the *Avodah* not being performed in the sequence written is because there is a *halakhah l'Moshe miSinai,* an oral tradition handed down from Moses at Sinai, that the *Kohen Gadol* must sanctify his hands and feet ten times and immerse himself five times during the ritual. If the Biblical description of the *Avodah* were to be followed in the written sequence, there would then be only six sanctifications and three immersions.

Therefore, if during his public Torah reading the *Kohen Gadol* were to publicly read only *Torah Shebikhtav* without inserting the clarifications from *Torah Sheb'al Peh*, there would be an inconsistency between his words and his actions. This divergence between the apparent *Torah Shebikhtav* description and the *Torah Sheb'al Peh* explanation was in fact one of the differences of opinion between the Pharisees and the Sadducees.[2]

During the seven-day sequester of the *Kohen Gadol* prior to Yom Kippur, he was required to review the laws pertaining to the *Avodah*. One rationale given in the Gemara for this halakhah (*Yoma* 2a) is that this sequester mirrors the seven days during which Moses taught Aaron the detail of the *Mishkan* service.[i] The Gemara states: "And two scholars of the students of Moshe Rabbeinu…taught him all seven days so as to educate him regarding the *Avodah* ritual" (*Yoma* 4a). Therefore, before the *Kohen Gadol*

---

[2] This disagreement is not mentioned specifically in the Gemara. The major disagreement between the Pharisees and the Sadducees, recorded in the Gemara in *Yoma* 53a, was whether the *Kohen Gadol* was to prepare the incense while in the Holy of Holies, or before entering there.

could perform the *Avodah*, he was first required to enter the *beit midrash*, the house of study, and study *Torah Sheb'al Peh* from those who transmitted the oral tradition, the "students of Moshe Rabbeinu." Seven days were required to teach the *Kohen Gadol* the laws within *Torah Sheb'al Peh* dealing with the *Avodah*.

Given the above, we must ask: Why is the *Avodah* ritual written so ambiguously that an apparent dichotomy exists between *Torah Shebikhtav* and *Torah Sheb'al Peh*? According to the Rav, these inconsistencies were introduced deliberately in order to teach us that *Torah Shebikhtav* without *Torah Sheb'al Peh* is in fact not Torah at all.

The reason an affirmation of the validity of *Torah Sheb'al Peh* plays such a conspicuous part in the Yom Kippur *Avodah* recitation is explained by the Rav's great grandfather, Reb Yosef Ber Soloveitchik *zt"l* (the *Beit HaLevi*).[3] He suggests that Yom Kippur is actually the day that *Torah Sheb'al Peh* was conferred on the Children of Israel .

The *Beit HaLevi* explains that in the giving of the Torah at Sinai on the first Shavuot, both *Torah Shebikhtav* and *Torah Sheb'al Peh* were committed to writing, and that in fact the first Tablets that Moses brought down from Sinai contained both in a coherent whole. However, as Moses observed the Children of Israel after the sin of the Golden Calf, in the words of the *Yalkut Shimoni* (*Ki Tisa* 393), "the words [on the Tablets] flew away." Clarifying this enigmatic statement, the *Beit HaLevi* explains that this refers to the *Torah Sheb'al Peh* portion having departed, leaving only *Torah Shebikhtav*. Because it is impossible to fulfill *Torah Shebikhtav* without the *Torah Sheb'al Peh* explication, this departure figuratively made the Tablets become heavy, causing Moses to drop them.

In contrast to the first set of Tablets, the second set, presented to the Children of Israel on Yom Kippur, contained only *Torah*

Shebikhtav, intending that *Torah Sheb'al Peh* be based solely on oral transmission. A passage in *Gittin* 60a quotes Rabbi Yoḥanan as follows: "The Holy One Blessed Be He did not make a covenant with Israel except for the sake of the oral transmission as the verse says, 'Through (in Hebrew *al pi*, homiletically translated as "orally") these words I have made with them a covenant.'" This verse appears in the Biblical narrative only at the giving of the second Tablets.[ii]

After the *Kohen Gadol*'s public reading on Yom Kippur, he said these words: "More than I have read to you is herein written" (*Mishnah Yoma* 7:1). In a homiletic interpretation, the Rav stated that within this phrase the *Kohen Gadol* indicated that there is an oral tradition that is integral to the *Avodah*. This is the key to understanding the reason for our own recitation of the *Avodah* during *Musaf*. The Torah portion that we read on Yom Kippur is insufficient to accurately describe the *Avodah*; by reciting the *Avodah*, we also demonstrate the indispensability of *Torah Sheb'al Peh*.

This affirmation continues as a central theme in our present-day *Avodah* recitation. *Attah Konanta*, the version of the *Avodah* service in the *Nusaḥ Sefard maḥzor*, was written during the period of the second *Beit Hamikdash*, and many in fact maintain that it was composed by the *Kohen Gadol* himself.[4] Its syntax and structure is that of the mishnah and *baraita*. The wording is clearly that of *Torah Sheb'al Peh*, and indeed constitutes a manifesto declaring faith in the authenticity of *Torah Sheb'al Peh*.[5]

---

[4] The Rav indicated that the *Nusaḥ Ashkenaz* version of the *Avodah* (*Amitz Ko'aḥ*) was composed much later and contains within it a few difficult passages which seem inconsistent with the *Avodah* service as it was actually practiced.

[5] Just as Yom Kippur is the holiday commemorating the giving of *Torah Sheb'al Peh*, Sukkot is the Yom Tov which actually celebrates *Torah Sheb'al Peh*. The Sadducees and Pharisees argued about very basic rules involving the Sukkot festival, e.g. *aravot, nisukh hamayim*. Indeed, what is

Ecstasy and Mourning

Besides the affirmation of *Torah Sheb'al Peh*, another motif is dominant in the *Avodah* recitation. The person reciting these *piyyutim* is placed in an almost beatific trance as he both observes and becomes involved in the ritual as it unfolds, compelled to follow every detail until its successful completion. In his 1979 *teshuvah derashah*, the Rav describes the recitation of the *Avodah* by his father and grandfather in this way:

> *They said it with so much enthusiasm, such ecstasy, that they could not stop. They were no longer in Warsaw or Brisk: they were transported to a different reality. Although I am not a musician or musicologist, all one had to do was hear the* nigun *[tune] of* Hakohanim Veha'am *to understand. One did not even need to hear the words in order to feel the nostalgia for what once existed and is no longer. Similarly,* Vekakh hayah moneh: aḥas, aḥas v'aḥas.... *Towards the end of the* Avodah, *when the scarlet thread turned white, the* piyyut *describes how the nation exuded happiness, expressing pleasure and delight, a feeling of closeness to Hashem: He is right beside me.*

The description of the *Avodah* culminates in the majestic *piyyut, Mar'eh Kohen*, which describes the luminous appearance of the *Kohen Gadol* after successfully completing the *Avodah*:

---

a sukkah? What should its height be? The vast majority of the halakhot of Sukkah are *halakhah l'Moshe miSinai*. Sukkot is therefore the festival of *Torah Sheb'al Peh*. At the same time Sukkot is the holiday wherein we celebrate the *taharat hanefesh* effected by Yom Kippur.
(וביום הראשון-ראשון לחשבון עוונות -מדרש תנחומא אמור כ'ב)

Why the happiness in reciting Mar'eh Kohen*? Why was it sung with such a happy tune? The answer is that the* Kohen Gadol *reflected the radiance of the* Shekhinah. *Through witnessing the radiant appearance of the* Kohen Gadol, *there could be no doubt about Hashem's acceptance of* Klal Yisrael's *prayers.*

The description of the Avodah itself is now complete. At this point, however, a new theme appears in the Yom Kippur prayer book. The refrain of the next *piyyut* reads: "Fortunate the eye which saw all these things; for the ear to hear of it distresses our soul." In the Rav's words:

Suddenly the liturgist and the reader of the piyyut *are rudely awakened from a dream.[6] They cry, "This is no longer the reality in which we live. It existed once, yes, but is no more." One finds himself alone on a stormy night, dark, lost, and he cries out, "All this occurred while the Temple was in existence; fortunate the eye which saw all these things." Fortunate the eye --- but not our eyes.*

While reciting the *Avodah*, the Jew was transported to a different, beautiful world. He is now rudely awakened to find himself in a bitter exile. The detail we just discussed: *vekakh hayah moneh, vekakh hayah omer, hakohanim veha'am...* we no longer have.

Immediately after the joy of reciting the *Avodah*, we recite *piyyutim* of mourning. Suddenly, Yom Kippur is transformed into a Tishah b'Av, the mourning reaching its most wrenching moment as

---

[6] The Rav's tone changed dramatically at this point in the *derashah*. His tone was foreboding, becoming almost bitter as he said these words.

we recount the story of the *asarah harugei malkhut*, the ten *tanna'im* martyred by the Romans.

Why *kinot* on Yom Kippur? Why the mourning? The *Yerushalmi* indicates that there is one sin a person must confront that does not appear in *vidui*: "Every generation in which the *Beit Hamikdash* is not built is as if it was destroyed by that same generation" (*Yerushalmi Yoma* 4b). The function of mourning on Yom Kippur is the recognition of sin, as it says in the *mahzor*: *aval avonoteinu he'erikhu kitzo,--* our sins have extended its state of destruction. In the introduction to *vidui* we say: "for we are not so brazen and obstinate to say before You, Hashem, our God and God of our forefathers, that we are righteous and have not sinned." It is impossible to deny that we have sinned, because we find ourselves at a time in which the *Beit Hamikdash* remains destroyed -- our sin stares us in the face. The relationship between the destruction of the *Beit Hamikdash* and our own sins is verbalized explicitly in *Selihot*:

> The residence of our Temple was destroyed through our sins; our palace was devastated, the beauty of our land was given to aliens, our strength to strangers. Yet we have still not turned back from our erroneous ways: how can we be so stubborn and stiff-necked to say to You that we are righteous and have not sinned...?

The startling contrast between the joy of the *Avodah* recitation and the pain evoked by reciting the *piyyutim* immediately following serves a basic cognitive purpose. In order to truly feel a loss, a person must internalize two key points: 1) how wonderful life was before the loss and 2) how terrible life is after the loss. In the words of Jeremiah: "Jerusalem remembered in the days of her affliction and of her miseries all her pleasant things that she had in the days of old" (Lamentations 1:7). To merely articulate our present plight is not a *kinah*. A born slave senses no deficiency in his life.[iii] In order to feel a loss one must first have experienced the "pleasant things." This is the point of reciting the *Avodah*: to feel the reality of the *Beit Hamikdash* which is no longer. This is the *kinah* a Jew says on Yom Kippur. The mourning that takes place on Yom Kippur is our recognition of sin.

Rabbi Akiva's Affirmation

However, the hope to attain the closeness to God characterized by the *Avodah* is not lost to contemporary man. The words of Rabbi Akiva at the end of *Mishnah Yoma* act as a ray of hope to our generation so far removed from the Temple service. Rabbi Akiva, in response to the feelings of hopelessness experienced by the Jewish people upon the Temple's destruction said: "Happy are you, Israel: before whom are you purified and who purifies you: your Father in Heaven." (*Mishnah Yoma* 8:9).

All the commentaries ask, "What is the significance of such a statement? Who else could purify us?" The answer lies in understanding the historical context of the statement. It was the first Yom Kippur after the Temple's destruction. The Jews could not conceive of the possibility of such a Yom Kippur: a Yom Kippur without the *Kohen Gadol*, *sa'ir la'azazel*, the Holy of Holies, a Yom Kippur based on one concept alone: individual repentance. The Jews were in pain and despair. How could there be a Yom Kippur without a *Beit Hamikdash*?

The response of Rabbi Akiva has been explained by the Rav in the following way:[7]

> Then rose Rabbi Akiva, the unswerving "optimist," and he said: There is no need for such mournfulness and helplessness. Indeed, we have been bereft of the Temple and its Divine dispensation of grace for the atonement of sin. But we have lost only *kapparah*, atonement and penitence, but not *taharah*, purification. Indeed,

---

[7] From *Sacred and Profane*. See also *On Repentance*, "Atonement and Purification."

we have been bereft of the ceremonies and sacrifices that are relevant to the transcendent act of the erasure of sin by supernatural grace and incomprehensible Divine benevolence that alter the past and disrupt the causal chain. The attainment of *kapparah* will not be as complete and perfect now as it was when the cult worship acts of the High Priest brought man into contact with transcendent and incomprehensible divinity. But we Jews have brought another message of *teshuvah* to man, that of *taharah*. There is nothing transcendent, miraculous, or non-rational about *taharah*...The performance of *taharah* is not directed at a transcendent divinity but at God, as our Father, Companion, and intimate Counselor...this communion of God - man has not been affected by the loss of outward ceremonial rites.

TESHUVAH AND REDEMPTION

Basing his presentation on an analysis of an anomalous juxtaposition of halakhot in the *Mishneh Torah*, the Rav quoted the following:

> Let it not seem that one who does *teshuvah* is distant from the level of the righteous because of the sins and transgressions that he has done. This is not true; rather he is loved and dear before the Creator as if he had never sinned, and additionally his reward is very great (*Hilkhot Teshuvah* 7:4).

> All the prophets unanimously commanded us to do *teshuvah*, and Israel will not be redeemed except through *teshuvah*, and the Torah has already promised that Israel will ultimately do *teshuvah* at the end of their exile... (*Hilkhot Teshuvah* 7:5).

> Great is *teshuvah*, for it brings a person close to the Divine Presence, as the verse states: "Return O Israel unto Hashem your G-d." Yesterday he was hated before the Omnipresent...and today he is loved, dear, close, and a friend (*Hilkhot Teshuvah* 7:6).

There is an inconsistency in the sequence of the above halakhot: the theme of individual redemption in the first halakhah cited above continues in the third, with the second halakhah discussing the redemption of all Israel. Why did the Rambam interrupt his development of the theme of individual *teshuvah* with that of communal *teshuvah* and national redemption?

There is a well-known axiom in life addressed in the Gemara (*Yoma* 29a): "It is more difficult to relearn something forgotten than to learn something new." It is harder to rebuild than to build from scratch. As one example, building a new business is accompanied with enthusiasm; rebuilding a bankrupt business is far more difficult. The Torah emphasizes the calamity of: "...if your brother becomes poor" (Leviticus 25:25). The misfortune of "becoming poor" as opposed to simply "being poor" is due to the experience of loss. In a similar vein, the tragedy behind old age is the necessity to relearn how to perform tasks and actions that were so facile when one was younger. We can attempt to build a substitute structure, but we can never restore the majesty of the original.

The axiom of the Gemara is graphically illustrated in the following quotation from Ezra, describing the conflicting response of the Jewish people upon the dedication of the second Temple:

> But many of the Priests and Levites and heads of fathers' houses, the old men that had seen the first Temple standing on its foundation, wept with a loud voice when this Temple was before their eyes, and many [others] shouted aloud for joy. So the people could not discern the sound of the shout of joy from the sound of the weeping of the people... (Ezra 3:12-13).

The first Temple surpassed the second in beauty. The revelation of Divine Presence in the first surpassed the second. The second contained no *Urim Vetumim*, no Ark of the Covenant, no heavenly fire. Those who remembered the majesty of the first structure were bitterly disappointed with the second.

Another example of the axiom is contained in the following Gemara in *Bava Batra:*

> The elders of that generation [i.e. the generation that witnessed the leadership pass from Moses to Joshua] would say that the countenance of Moses was like that of the sun, [while] the countenance of Joshua was like that of the moon. Woe for this shame, woe for this disgrace (*Bava Batra* 75a).

The shame mentioned here is the tragedy of a new leader who does not measure up to the first. The priests perceived that the new generation of leadership would be but a mere reflection of the previous generation.

The Rav mentioned yet another example of incomplete reconstruction on a national level. During the ingathering of the exiles under Ezra, the land that was under Israel's control before the Babylonian dispersion was not completely restored; the territory was much smaller. "There are many areas [in Israel] that those who came up from Egypt conquered, that those who came up from Babylonia did not conquer" (*Ḥagigah* 3b). There are halakhic implications to this loss of status in the second exilic ingathering. The Rambam maintains that in the time of Ezra the laws of tithes, of *terumah* and *ma'aser*, were only Rabbinic in origin in contrast to the situation prior to the Babylonian exile.[8] The *Kohen Gadol* was not anointed with the special oil set aside for this purpose.[9] Interestingly, the fast of Tishah b'Av was actually observed during the second Temple period because of the incomplete restoration of the Temple.[10]

---

[8] Rambam, *Hilkhot Terumot* 1:26.

[9] Rambam, *Hilkhot Klei Hamikdash* 1:8.

[10] *Megillah* 5a.

Yet, in contrast to man, one characteristic of Hashem is the ease with which he effects complete restoration.[11]   To Hashem, rebuilding is as facile as building, and herein lies the difference between the return of Ezra to Israel and the final redemption. The final redemption will be a complete one. Everything that existed in the desert Tabernacle will be restored: "Then shall the offering of Judah and Jerusalem be pleasant unto Hashem as in the days of old as in former years" (Malachi 3:4).

For this reason, the Rambam states:

> The King Messiah will in the future erect and restore the kingdom of the House of David to its original splendor, will build Jerusalem, ingather the dispersed of Israel, and ingather all the tribes as they were originally, offering sacrifices and establishing sabbaticals and jubilees in accordance with all laws stated in the Torah (*Hilkhot Melakhim* 11:1).

The Rambam here formulates three criteria for complete national restoration: political/military renaissance, Temple reconstruction, and restoration of mitzvot dependent on the Land of Israel.[12]

What then is the relationship between national and individual renewal and redemption as implied by the Rambam's juxtaposition of the halakhot cited above? According to Rav Ḥaim Volozhin, there is no truer Temple than the personality of the individual.[13] The Biblical verse states: "And they will make me a Tabernacle and I will dwell within <u>them</u>" (Exodus 25:8). The Divine Presence

---

[11]The phrase, בניתי הנהרסות -- I have restored the ruins (Ezekiel 36:36) reflects this attribute.

[12] These mitzvot include *terumah* and *ma'aser*, *shemitah* and *yovel*. Most Rishonim hold that there was no Biblically mandated *shmitah* and *yovel* during the second Temple period (with the exception of *Tosafot* [*Yevamot* 82b s.v. *yerushah rishonah*]).

[13] נפש החיים-שער א פרק ד

resides within us. Conversely, sin involves the removal of God's presence from within the individual. Because sin is equated to the destruction of the Temple, in a very real sense a sinner does to himself what the tyrants Nevuzaraden and Titus did to the two Temples.

If sin is equated with destruction, one can then infer that *teshuvah* is equivalent to reconstruction. Yet what type of reconstruction does *teshuvah* achieve?

A Gemara in *Yoma* mentions the incomplete "second Temple" type of *teshuvah*: "Great is *teshuvah* for it brings healing to the world" (*Yoma* 86a), to which Rashi comments: "Like one blemished who is healed with a small vestige [of the disease] remaining."

In contrast, there are other passages in the same portion of Gemara that mention the "third Temple" type of *teshuvah*, a *teshuvah* involving total purification of the personality:

> R. Yohanan said: Great is *teshuvah* for it displaces a negative command in the Torah, as it states (Jeremiah 3:1): "They say, if a man sends away his wife and she goes from him and becomes another man's, shall he return to her again? Shall not that land be greatly polluted? You have played harlot with many lovers, yet return again to Me."

In light of the above, the juxtaposition of halakhot in the Rambam regarding individual and national renewal can be understood. In his discussion of individual *teshuvah*, the Rambam is clearly referring to the third Temple type of *teshuvah*, since he states that for one who performs *teshuvah*, the personality is restored to the previously exalted level. Thus after introducing this concept, and even before completing his thought, the Rambam asserts that the same miracle of total reconstruction will be part of Jewish history. If the Jewish people properly summon their power of free will and becomes their own personal redeemer, then Hashem will respond in kind by providing us national redemption through a Messiah who in turn will accomplish the same miracle of complete communal reconstruction.[iv]

Today, *teshuvah* replaces the elaborate Temple ritual that at one time effected atonement. A person must therefore strive to achieve the complete third Temple type of *teshuvah* in order for atonement to be complete.

MINḤAH: THE HOPE FOR UNIVERSAL ATONEMENT

In the *Minḥah* service (the afternoon prayer) of Yom Kippur, we read the Book of Jonah as the *Haftarah* portion. One reason that this portion is read at this particular time is because it illustrates the efficacy of repentance. Even after Hashem decided to punish the population of the city of Nineveh, His attribute of strict justice yielded to His attribute of mercy in response to their *teshuvah*. There is no clearer Biblical account of the potency of repentance.

Yet the Rav posits a second reason that this *Haftarah* portion is read precisely at this point in the service. Throughout the day of Yom Kippur as well as the previous evening, our supplications until this point in the service are exclusively limited to Israel's needs. Our prayers and confessions are limited in scope to requesting forgiveness for ourselves and our community. We have not prayed for mankind as a whole.

The contrast between Israel and the rest of mankind is turned up to an extreme in the Torah portion read at *Minḥah*: the portion dealing with illicit sexual relationships.[14] The key message of this

---

[14] Various *Rishonim*, including *Tosafot* and the Rambam, strain to find an appropriate explanation for reading this specific portion of the Torah at this point. *Tosafot* (*Megillah* 31a s.v. *lo beminḥah*) explains that because the women are dressed in their finery in honor of the holiday, the temptation is great to engage in such relationships. The Rambam (*Hilkhot Tefillah* 13:11) explains that this portion is read at this point simply to remind us of sin in order to prompt *teshuvah*.

particular passage in the Torah is given in the introductory verse: "Like the practices of the land of Egypt in which you once lived, you are not to do, and like the practices of the land of Canaan to which I bring you, you are not to do..." (Leviticus 18:3).

This portion of the Torah is read on Yom Kippur so that we internalize this essential directive. Israel is separate and distinct from the nations surrounding her. We must uphold this unique identity and under no conditions are we to consider assimilation. Egypt and Canaan are mentioned specifically because these nations represented the two poles of secular civilization in Biblical times. Egypt was the most urbanized and technologically advanced civilization of the time, while Canaan was pastoral and primitive. The Torah emphasizes here that as different as they were from each other, neither of these fundamentally immoral societies should serve as role models.

Throughout Jewish history, the principle of our separation from the nations, of our particularity, has been imbued in our consciousness. The State of Israel was established with this principle in mind. Even today, which nation is as abandoned, as alone, as the State of Israel? The essential message of the Torah reading on *Minḥah* of Yom Kippur is that if we do not separate from the nations, we can become corrupt and impure.

Yet, if a Jew exclusively internalizes the message of the Torah reading without considering the *Haftarah*, he will have missed another key message of Yom Kippur.

As the end of the day approaches, we remember that we Jews are not alone. We recount a tale of *teshuvah*, not of an Israelite tribe, but of an Assyrian city whose population actually harbored hatred for Israel. Yet, the gates of repentance are open to all people, Jews and non-Jews alike. The entire world needs *teshuvah*.

On Yom Kippur we begin by praying for Israel alone, but towards the end of the day, we include the rest of humanity.[v] This is the Jewish approach towards the non-Jew. We must maintain our uniqueness but, at the same time, we must not forget the non-Jew.

The same paradox of separation and inclusiveness regarding the non-Jew is a theme on Passover, on Seder night. Is there any holiday that better symbolizes the theme of separation? The nations have oppressed us through interminable exiles. How can a Jew possibly recite: "We were slaves to Pharaoh in Egypt" on Passover night, and at the same time consider Pharaoh as a brother? The blessing we say is: "Blessed art Thou...Who has redeemed Israel." One lifts his cup and says, *ve'hi she'amdah*, a passage suggesting total separation from the nations. Throughout the initial parts of the Seder we repeat these themes again and again.

Yet towards the Seder's conclusion, after we have eaten our matzah and are about to recite the blessing on the fourth cup of wine, we say: "The soul of every being shall bless Your Name, Hashem our God, the spirit of all flesh shall always glorify and exalt Your remembrance."

On Pesaḥ, we pray not only for our redemption, but for the redemption of mankind. Similarly, on Yom Kippur, we pray not only for our own atonement, but for the atonement of mankind as well.

NEI'LAH: ACCEPTANCE OF PRAYER

While in the days of the Temple the *Avodah* service was considered synonymous with the Yom Kippur experience, today our own cognitive association with Yom Kippur is that of a day devoted entirely to prayer. According to the Rav, prayer on Yom Kippur takes on a complexion fundamentally different from prayer the rest of the year. The day of Yom Kippur must be transformed into a *yom tefillah,* a day of prayer. To accomplish this transformation, the Rabbis instituted the *Ne'ilah* service. The purpose of *Ne'ilah* is to request that all the previous prayers of the day be accepted before God.

This conception of the role of the *Ne'ilah* service was so compelling to the Rav that he actually posited a halakhah on this basis.[vi] If during the year one forgets to pray any of the three daily prayers (*Shaḥarit, Minḥah*, or *Ma'ariv*) in their proper time, it does not affect one's halakhic ability to participate in subsequent prayers. However, according to the Rav, if for some reason one did not pray on Yom Kippur until the time for *Ne'ilah* has arrived, he may not participate in the *Ne'ilah* service. The function of *Ne'ilah* is to transform all previous prayers into one unified prayer activity. Without the earlier prayers there can be no *Ne'ilah*.

On the eve of Yom Kippur, immediately following the *Amidah* of *Ma'ariv*, we recite the *piyyut* called *Ya'aleh*, a *piyyut* which apprehends the unique nature of prayer on Yom Kippur: "May our supplications ascend from evening, and may our cry arrive from morning, and may our praise find favor (literally, 'be seen') by evening." Through anticipation of *Ne'ilah* from the previous evening, we request that the entire day be a *yom tefillah*.

All three verbs in this first sentence of the *piyyut* are paralleled by the Biblical description of three stages in Israel's prayer during the Egyptian exile. There are three parts to the *piyyut*:

1) *Evening -- Ascension*: Th₌ Torah describes the initial stage of prayer by the enslaved Hebrews: "...˄nd t::˄r cry ascended unto God by reason of the bondage" (Exodus 2:23). At ᶜ₌₌ point in their slavery experience, Israel had no intention of formulating prayer as such. This initial stage of prayer was little more than a poorly articulated, instinctive cry.[vii] According to the Ramban, Hashem Himself "lifted" their groaning, allowing their cry to rise up before Him. On the evening of Yom Kippur, we similarly ask Hashem to allow our prayer to ascend.

2) *Morning – Arrival:* "...the cry of the Children of Israel has come before Me" (Exodus 3:9). In the morning we ask Hashem that our prayer enter before Him and be heard.

3) *Evening -- Acceptance ("seeing")*: "...and God saw...and took cognizance..." (Exodus 2:25). *Ne'ilah* is the prayer service in which we ask for Hashem's acceptance of all our prayers, uniting

all the previous prayers into one large *ma'aseh tefillah* or prayer activity.

The *piyyut* therefore expresses the hope that our prayers of the evening become a suitable introduction to those of the morning, and that those of the morning be a suitable introduction to those of the following evening, in accordance with the Biblical verse regarding Yom Kippur:

> "...from evening until evening you shall keep this Sabbath"
> (Leviticus 23:32).

NOTES

[i] In a *Yarḥei Kallah* lecture on the subject of the Yom Kippur *Avodah* (1971), the Rav expanded on this theme. During this seven-day prelude, the *Kohen Gadol* experiences two fundamental changes of his personal status. On one level, the seven days elevates the *Kohen Gadol* until he is the virtual personification of Aaron himself. For this reason the Biblical *Avodah* description refers specifically to tasks that Aaron was to perform (i.e. בזאת יבוא אהרן אל הקודש) rather than a generalized description of the *Kohen Gadol*'s duties. On a second level, the *Kohen Gadol* becomes transformed into a holy Temple vessel, as he was required to use his hands to transfer incense from the ladle to the shovel while in the Holy of Holies. The seven-day period of *Avodah* preparation thus facilitates both transformations. (See *Nora'ot Harav*, Vol. 6, pp. 54-56 and 70-74.)

[ii] The *Beit HaLevi* further explains the reason that *Torah Sheb'al Peh* was presented orally only after the first Tablets were broken. According to a passage in *Eruvin* 54a, had the sin of the Golden Calf not take place and the Tablets not been broken, Israel would never have experienced the yoke of foreign domination. However, once having sinned, Israel became vulnerable to outside conquest. God foresaw that these nations would then expropriate Israel's religious texts as their own. Hence, by keeping this portion of the Torah away from Scripture, *Torah Sheb'al Peh* remained the unique possession of Israel.

[iii] See Redemption, Prayer and Talmud Torah, *Tradition* (June 1978):

> The animal is exposed to pain; so is the slave. When the slave meets with pain he reacts like the animal, uttering a sharp shrill sound. However, the howl of the beast, like the shriek of the slave, lasts a moment in the darkness and the hush of the night. In a split second all is silent again. There is no aftermath to the pain sensation of the animal or the slave; there follows no complaint, no request, no protest, no question of why and what. The slave does not know suffering, lacking, as he does, the very existential need awareness, which generates suffering.

[iv] The same theme of the relationship between individual and national renewal is explored further in *On Repentance*, "Expiation, Suffering and Redemption".

[v] The motif of the *Zikhronot* section recited in *Musaf* of Rosh Hashanah reflects this theme of universal *teshuvah*. We recount how Hashem remembered Noah as he was saved from the flood, and we also recite "אשרי איש שלא ישכחך," in which all people are encouraged to repent (1970 *Yarḥei Kallah*).

[vi] See:

מסורה,חוברת ו,כסלו תשנ'ב ("מפי השמועה ממרן הגרי"ד סולוביצ'יק")

ביסוד ענין הסליחות:

כ"ה בירושלמי דיסוד ענין תפילת נעילה היינו - ריבוי תפילה, והמקור לזה מהפסוק "גם כי תרבו תפילה אינני שומע","יש יותר סיכויים שייענה לחיוב, ובתענית שהוא יום צרה- בעינן ריבוי תפילה. והיה נראה לומר שאם אחד הי ' ישן כל יום הכיפורים ולא התפלל לא שחרית ולא מוסף ולא מנחה, ובא לביהכ"נ בסוף היום בשעה שמתפללים נעילה, שאין לו להתפלל נעילה עמהם דגדר ענין נעילה היינו - ריבוי תפילה ובלא התפלל כל שאר תפילות היום אין מקום כלל להתפלל תפילת נעילה . ובזה הי' הג"ר משה סלאוויצ'יק ז"ל מסופק אם די במה שהתפלל אחת מתפילות היום. ולרבינו שיחי' הי' נראה עפ"י פשוטו דלא חשיבא תפילת הנעילה בבחינת ריבוי תפילה אא" כ התפלל <u>לכל שאר</u> תפילות היום, והוסיף תפילה זו עליהן.

[vii] See Redemption, Prayer and Talmud Torah, *Tradition* (June 1978):

Moses, by defending the helpless Jew, restored sensitivity to the dull slaves. Suddenly they realized that all that pain, anguish, humiliation, and cruelty...is evil. This realization brought in its wake not only sharp pain, but a sense of suffering as well. With suffering came loud protest, the cry...The dead silence of non-existence was gone; the voice of human existence was now heard....It is in this second stage, with the awakening of the need-awareness, that prayer makes its entry. This level of intermediate prayer is not yet *tefillah* but *tze'akah*, a human outcry... there is not yet a clear understanding of what one is crying for... *Tze'akah* is primordial prayer, the voice restored, the word still lacking.

References

English:

Besdin, Abraham R. 1993. *Reflections of the Rav*: Volume 1 (Revised Edition). Hoboken, New Jersey: KTAV Publishing House Inc.

Epstein, Joseph, ed. 1974. *Shiurei Harav: A Conspectus of the Public Lectures of Rabbi Joseph B. Soloveitchik.* New York: *Hamevaser - The Official Student Publication of the Jewish Studies Division of Yeshiva University.*

Peli, Pinchas H. *On Repentance in the Thought and Oral Discourse of Rabbi Joseph B. Soloveitchik.* Jerusalem: Oroth Publishing House, 1980; Northvale, New Jersey: Jason Aronson Inc., 1996.

Schreiber, B. David, ed. 1997-8. *Nora'ot Harav*: Volumes 1, 5, and 6. Distributed by Rabbi Yaakov Levitz, Brooklyn, NY.

Soloveitchik, Joseph B. 5726/1966. "Sacred and Profane: *Kodesh* and *Chol* in World Perspectives." *Gesher – A Publication of the Student Organization of Yeshiva University* 3:1 (Sivan/June): 5-29.

Soloveitchik, Joseph B. 1978. "Redemption, Prayer, Talmud Torah" *Tradition: A Journal of Orthodox Jewish Thought* 17:2 (Spring) 55-72.

Soloveitchik, Joseph B. 1983. *Halakhic Man,* Philadelphia: Jewish Publication Society.

Soloveitchik, Joseph B. 1992. *"Kol Dodi Dofek*: It Is the Voice of My Beloved That Knocketh," in B.H. Rosenberg and F. Heuman, eds. *Theological and Halakhic Reflections on the Holocaust.* Hoboken, New Jersey: Ktav Publishing House Inc.

Telsner, David, ed. 1983. *The Rav Speaks: Five Addresses by Rabbi Joseph B. Soloveitchik.* Jerusalem: Tal Orot Institute.

Ziegler, Aharon. 1998. *Halachic Positions of Rabbi Joseph B. Soloveitchik.* Northvale, New Jersey: Jason Aronson Inc.

Hebrew:

אליעזר גולדמן, "תשובה וזמן בהגות הרב סולובייצ'יק." *אמונה בזמנים משתנים: על משנתו של הרב י.ד. סולובייצ'יק,* נערך ע"י אבי שגיא. ירושלים: ספריית אלינר - ההסתדרות הציונית העולמית ומרכז יעקב הרצוג, תשנ'ז.

הרב יוסף דוב הלוי סולובייצ'יק, "על אהבת התורה וגאולת נפש הדור ", *בסוד היחיד והיחד,* נערך ע'י פנחס פלאי, ירושלים: אורות, תשל'ו

הרב יוסף דוב הלוי סולובייצ'יק, "ובקשתם משם", ו'רעיונות על התפילה." *איש ההלכה-גלוי ונסתר,* נערך ע'י משה קרונה. ירושלים: ההסתדרות הציונית העולמית, תשל'ט.

הרב יוסף דוב הלוי סולובייצ'יק, שיעורים לזכר אבא מרי ז"ל. ירושלים: עקיבא יוסף, תשמ'ג.

מסורה-מאסף תורני ע"י מחלקת הכשרות של איחוד הקהילות החרדיות באמריקה (ניו יורק): *מפי השמועה ממרן הגרי"ד סולובייצ'יק--* כרך ב'- *בענין אין יוה"כ מכפר עד שירצה את חבירו,* דף כג, (תשרי תש'ן); כרך ו'- *ביסוד ענין הסליחות,* דף כב (כסלו תשנ'ב).

משה קרונה, ימי זכרון, ירושלים: ההסתדרות הציונית העולמית, תשמ'ז.

Appendix

דבר שבקדושה as a קריאת שמע*

Twice every day, the classic affirmation of faith, קריאת שמע, is recited in our prayers. Immediately subsequent to the first line, before reciting the remainder of the Biblical passage, we say the phrase (בשכמל"ו) ברוך שם כבוד מלכותו לעולם ועד. The גמרא in .נז פסחים states the halakhah that although the first line is said loudly, the second should be read quietly. The פרקי דרב אליעזר explains that when Moses received the Torah on Har Sinai, he heard the angels reciting that particular verse quietly, and as a result, we maintain that practice today.

Yet, the *Shulhan Arukh* cites an ancient tradition from Ashkenaz that on Yom Kippur בשכמל"ו is said aloud. Again, there are some aggadic reasons provided, but the Rav said that he preferred to explain the reason for the dichotomy on precise halakhic grounds.

There are a number of passages in the daily prayers that have a special status known as דבר שבקדושה. Included in this category are קדושה and ברכו. The main halakhah regarding a דבר שבקדושה is that a minyan is required in order for one to be permitted to recite it. On the basis of this simple rule, one would reach the conclusion that קריאת שמע is not a דבר שבקדושה since it can indeed be recited without a minyan. Although we affirm the יחוד ה' through its

---

* BASED ON THE 1978 *TESHUVAH DERASHAH*

recitation, we perform this mitzvah through a simple reading of the Biblical text, not as a public proclamation.[1]

A central feature of any דבר שבקדושה is the specific role of the שליח ציבור in prompting responses from the congregation. קדושה is a responsive exercise, with the שליח ציבור announcing and the congregation responding. This activity mimics the angels, as each prompts the other to respond: ונותנים רשות זה לזה. Each member of the community, be they angels or men, asks permission of one another to make the declaration. It is therefore axiomatic that a דבר שבקדושה be read aloud.

Within the קדושה of מוסף we do in fact recite the first sentence of קריאת שמע specifically as a דבר שבקדושה. In this context, שמע ישראל ה' אלוקינו ה' אחד becomes transformed from a private reading to a public דבר שבקדושה proclamation.

To buttress the contrast between the recitation of קריאת שמע the remainder of the year versus קריאת שמע on Yom Kippur, the Rav related that he once asked his father to ask his grandfather, Reb Ḥaim Soloveitchik *zt"l*, whether or not one is allowed to say בשכמל"ו aloud after reading the first line of קריאת שמע. R. Ḥaim answered that as an individual praying alone, one may recite this passage as loudly as one wants. However, within a minyan it would be prohibited to read בשכמל"ו aloud, since the recitation of שמע קריאת would thus be converted to a דבר שבקדושה.

Why indeed are we not allowed to make such a conversion? The answer lies in examining the concept of קדושה itself. קדושה is Biblically depicted as the song of angels, שירת המלאכים. We invoke the angels' proclamation in the introductory stanza of the קדושה: נקדש את שמך בעולם כשם שמקדישים אותו בשמי מרום -- "We will sanctify Your Name in the world just as the [angels] sanctify it in the upper

---

[1] Other mitzvot that similarly involve an affirmation of God's unity, but are said בתורת קריאה rather than as a דבר שבקדושה include וידוי מעשרות and מקרא ביכורים.

heavens." The angels are invoked because lowly man requires special sanction to recite קדושה. This sanction is based on the fact that the angels' proclamation appears within the written Torah. Torah was provided freely to the nation: (במדבר כ״יח) וממדבר מתנה. We are therefore allowed to freely recite any Biblical passage aloud.

However, the phrase בשכמל״ו does not appear in תורה שבכתב. Therefore, when praying with a minyan, בשכמל״ו is only allowed to be said in an undertone, since aloud it would transform קריאת שמע into an unauthorized דבר שבקדושה.

The one day in the year that בשכמל״ו may be said aloud is Yom Kippur, because on Yom Kippur alone, קריאת שמע indeed becomes a דבר שבקדושה. The Rav brought a proof for this assertion from a *piyyut* that is recited on Yom Kippur just after the שירת המלאכים prior to קריאת שמע. The first two lines of the *piyyut* read as follows:

קדוש אדיר בעליתו..-- ברוך שם כבוד מלכותו לעולם ועד
קדוש בתשובה שת סליחתי -- ברוך שם כבוד מלכותו לעולם ועד

According to the Rav, the entire *piyyut* serves the halakhic function of transforming קריאת שמע into a דבר שבקדושה. Each stanza of this *piyyut* starts with the word קדוש and ends with the refrain בשכמל״ו. The שירת המלאכים, which reflects a דבר שבקדושה, forms the introduction to this *piyyut*. Thus, this *piyyut* heralds the imminent recitation of קריאת שמע as a דבר שבקדושה.[2]

What then is the היתר behind this transformation, given that בשכמל״ו, unlike שירת המלאכים, is not part of תורה שבכתב? The answer is that בשכמל״ו was the response of the people to the שם

---

[2] Although there is generally an obligation to stand during those prayers that have a status of דבר שבקדושה, קריאת שמע on Yom Kippur is the one exception. This is due to the phrase ובלכתך בדרך which proscribes standing during the recitation of קריאת שמע.

המפורש as intoned by the כהן גדול during the עבודה ritual. The שם
המפורש was the medium of public atonement during the time of the
Temple, with בשכמל"ו as the communal דבר שבקדושה response.

Thus the verse of שמע ישראל is a דבר שבקדושה every שבת ויום טוב
within the קדושה of מוסף, and קריאת שמע is likewise transformed
into a דבר שבקדושה every Yom Kippur. Similarly, בשכמל"ו at the
culmination of נעילה is recited aloud three times because the entire
character of נעילה is בתורת קדושה.

Rabbi Soloveitchik on the Days of Awe

Index

INDEX

CITATIONS

Tanakh

Talmud

Mishneh Torah (Maimonides)

Halakha/ Aggadah/ Other Sources

Orah Haim
582:1   6
597   14
619 (Tur)   74, 132
619   84

Yorah Deah
109 (Tur)   95
198:1   96

Yalkut Shimoni
Bereshit 20   4
Ki Tisa 393   41, 146
Nevi'im 529   91

Bereshit Rabba
3:8   124
8:1   44

Medrash Tanhuma
Emor 22   148

Zohar
Pinhas 131b   13

After attending Mesivta at the Talmudical Yeshiva of Philadelphia, Dr. Lustiger received a Ph.D. in Materials Science from Drexel University and is presently a Senior Polymer Scientist at Exxon Research and Engineering. Dr. Lustiger has previously published a summary of the Rav's work in *Jewish Action* and has written other summaries that were widely circulated on *mail.jewish,* a halakhah-oriented Internet mailing list. Dr. Lustiger resides in Edison, New Jersey with his wife Janice and their three children, Akiva, Noam, and Rena.